101 MORE GAMES FOR TRAINERS

Another Collection of the Best Activities from *Creative Training Techniques Newsletter*

By Bob Pike with Christopher Busse

QUANTITY SALES

Most Lakewood books are available at special quantity discounts when purchased in bulk by companies, organizations and special-interest groups. Custom imprinting or excerpting can also be done to fit special needs. For details contact Lakewood Books.

■   ■   ■

LAKEWOOD BOOKS
50 South Ninth Street
Minneapolis, MN 55402
(800) 328-4329 or (612) 333-0471
FAX (612) 333-6526

Publisher: Philip G. Jones
Editors: Bob Pike with Christopher Busse
Art Director/Production Editor: Julie Tilka
Print Production: Pat Grawert
Cover Design and Illustrations: George Peters

10 9 8 7 6 5 4 3

Lakewood Publications, Inc., publishes *TRAINING Magazine; Training Directors' Forum Newsletter; Creative Training Techniques Newsletter; The Lakewood Report Newsletter; Potentials In Marketing* Magazine; *Presentations Magazine;* and other business periodicals, books, research, and conferences.

Bob Pike, Creative Training Techniques International, 7620 W. 78th St., Edina, MN 55439, (612) 829-1960, fax (612) 829-0260.

ISBN 0-943210-44-5

FOREWORD

This book, *101 More Games for Trainers*, is one in a series drawn from the best content of *Creative Training Techniques Newsletter*. The newsletter was conceived in 1988 by editor and internationally known trainer Bob Pike to be a one-stop resource of practical "how-tos" for trainers. The idea was (and still is) to provide timely tips, techniques, and strategies that help trainers with the special tasks they perform daily.

When the newsletter began, it was largely fueled by Bob's 20 years of experience in the field and by the best ideas shared by the trainers (more than 50,000 in all) who had attended his Creative Training Techniques seminars. As the newsletter grew in popularity, it also began to draw on ideas submitted by its readers. Today, the newsletter continues to search out creative approaches from the more than 200 seminars Bob and the other Creative Training Techniques trainers conduct every year, and from the more than 10,000 newsletter readers.

But no matter where the insights originate, the goal of the newsletter remains the same: To provide trainers a cafeteria of ideas they can quickly absorb, choosing those that best suit their special needs.

This series of books represents the best ideas from *Creative Training Techniques Newsletter's* seven years of publication. It is our hope we've created a valuable resource you'll come back to again and again to help address the unique challenges you face daily in your role as a trainer.

Sincerely,

The Editors

INTRODUCTION

Like it or not, the age of entertainment in which we live demands that classroom trainers must work hard to capture and *hold* the interest of participants. If we don't, we run the risk of being passed by in favor of "sexier" learning methods, such as high-tech computer- or video-based training.

Fortunately, trainers have long known that one of the best ways to entertain and engage adult learners is to encourage them to play games in the classroom. And one advantage we have over any of the high-tech mediums that are capturing the attention of "cyber-trainees" is that we're able to adapt the courses and the games we offer to match precisely the needs of our audience. We can assess participants, decide what kind of an exercise is appropriate (and *when* it's appropriate), and use games that will ensure trainees are entertained...and course material is retained.

That's where *101 More Games for Trainers* comes in. Carefully selected and properly implemented, the exercises in this new volume (a companion to the earlier *101 Games for Trainers*) can help you actively involve trainees in course openers, bring a weary group back to life, develop communication skills, promote teamwork, lead an audience through a spirited review session, or address the special concerns of certain topical courses.

A brief description of its purpose is provided with each exercise, as well as a reference for the amount of time the exercise will take, the ideal group size for the exercise, and a checklist of materials you'll need to make the exercise happen. And because these represent the best of the ideas collected in *Creative Training Techniques Newsletter*, you know they've been successfully "field tested" all over the world by trainers just like you.

Defining the Categories

The exercises in this book fall into one or more of these six categories. Just below the title of each exercise, you'll find a listing of these six categories. The small check marks beside each of the categories serve as guides for where best to use the exercise.

Please remember, however, that these are only suggestions. With the right amount of imagination, the exercises here can be adapted to suit almost any training need.

Openers

These exercises, commonly known as "ice breakers," serve as vehicles for getting participants to introduce themselves or for putting trainees into the right "frame of mind" for the coming session.

These exercises may vary according to the type of training being conducted, how big the group is, and how well the group members know each other.

Also keep in mind the Law of Primacy: People remember what we do first, best. So choose your openers carefully. (To be honest, nearly all of the exercises here could be adapted as some form of opener.)

Energizers

Designed to involve a group *actively*, these midcourse exercises are best used during the infamous midafternoon slump or anytime you feel a group's attention might be waning.

Often, these games take the form of energetic review sessions or stimulating brainteasers, or even a physical activity that gets people up and moving. The secret here is that these exercises aren't always planned.

The best strategy in developing a course is to have a handful of relevant energizers ready to go at a moment's notice and implement one when you see attention begin to slip.

Communication

Use these exercises to make a point to trainees about the importance of communication, or to show where certain communication skills need improvement. Exercises that help enhance listening skills also fall into this category. As with "Openers," a great many of the activities in this book could easily be adapted to make a point about communication skills, depending upon how you position them.

Team-building

The purpose of these exercises is to help improve the relationship of individuals within a group — either a specific "work group" or simply a small group formed during your training session. These exercises are extremely challenging for trainers because they call for participants to work independently in small groups (usually solving some sort of problem) for periods of time that exceed other types of exercises. Your challenge is to keep things moving and to monitor closely the progress of the groups.

Review

The last words any group of trainees wants to hear are, "Okay, let's review." To keep participants from completely tuning out, these exercises often help disguise a review session as a light, interactive competition. *One word of caution:* When the competitive juices of some attendees get flowing, things can easily get out of hand. Your challenge is to keep the competition light and — whenever possible — to promote *cooperation* rather than competition.

Topical

One of the challenges trainers face is finding games and exercises that pertain to a certain kind of session (customer service or diversity training, for example). While many other exercises can be adapted for those kinds of training, we've identified several "topical" games that work particularly well in specific situations.

A Few Words About Using These Games

Whether it's the first or five hundredth time you've used games in your classroom, I believe there are some fundamentals you should be aware of when implementing these exercises.

▼ **Assess your audience and know the risks.** Some of the following exercises will be natural hits with certain types of audiences, others may bomb. Ultimately, it's up to you to decide what kind of game to play with what kind of audience.

But you also need to assess your own comfort level with "pulling off" these games. A rule of thumb: If you're even *remotely* uncomfortable with an exercise, don't use it. Trainees will sense your hesitation and share your discomfort.

▼ **Never use a game without debriefing afterward.** It may be obvious to *you* how a game enhances your subject matter, but it's dangerous to assume your participants are on the same page. Follow every game with a debriefing session to help trainees ease back into the session itself, see the transition you've attempted to create, and assimilate the game's learning points.

▼ **Be creative. Adapt, adapt, adapt.** Nothing about *any* game in this book is set in stone. The trainers to whom these ideas are attributed were successful in using these games because they adapted the exercises to suit their own needs.

Though you'll be able to pluck many of them right off the page and insert them into your sessions, I challenge you to make these games uniquely your own whenever you can. The result will be an exercise that has even more relevance to you, your company, and your classroom. But most important, the result will be an exercise that's more *fun*.

Bob Pike

CONTENTS

Game Categories:	Opener = O	Team-building = T-B
	Energizer = E	Review = R
	Communication = C	Topical = T

101 More Games for Trainers

Game Categories:	Opener = O			Team-building = T-B		
	Energizer = E			Review = R		
	Communication = C			Topical = T		

Game Categories:	☐ Opener	☐ Team-building
	☐ Energizer	☑ Review
	☐ Communication	☐ Topical:

■ **Purpose:** To engage participants creatively in a review of course material.

■ **Time Required:** 15 to 20 minutes.

■ **Size of Group:** Unlimited, but trainees should play the game in teams of three to six.

■ **Materials Required:** Index-sized "question cards," prepared in advance by the trainer. Small "service" bells for as many as there are teams (the type found at service counters).

■ **The Exercise in Action:** Prior to class, Bob Parsons, a training coordinator with Deluxe Corp. of Shoreview, MN, prepares a list of 26 questions and answers related to course material — one for each letter of the alphabet — and writes the question on the back of index cards, each with a different letter on the front.

He splits the class into teams and gives each team a bell. He lists the letters on a flip-chart page, and has teams take turns selecting letters. As they select letters, Parsons crosses off that letter from the flip chart and reads the corresponding card.

The first team to "ring in" tries to answer the question (if that answer is wrong, the first team to recognize that and ring in again gets a shot at it). When a question is answered correctly, Parsons hands the card to the successful team.

In its shortened version, the game ends when all 26 questions have been read, with prizes going to the team with the most cards. If time permits, Parsons allows five minutes for the teams to spell as many course-related words as possible, beginning with only the letters they've earned. He awards prizes to the team with the longest list.

TIP #2: Autobiographical Scavenger Hunt

Game Categories:

☑ **Opener**   ☐ **Team-building**
☑ **Energizer**   ☐ **Review**
☐ **Communication**   ☐ **Topical:**

■ **Purpose:** To break the ice and help introduce trainees to one another.

■ **Time Required:** 15 minutes.

■ **Size of Group:** Unlimited.

■ **Materials Required:** A list of autobiographical information for each trainee, prepared in advance by the trainer.

■ **The Exercise in Action:** Dale Ditmanson, training specialist for the National Park Service, asks participants to send in an "autobiography" before his courses. As an course opener, he selects a line or two from each autobiography and types them as a list.

Each participant is given a copy of the list as they arrive, then sent on a "human scavenger hunt" in the classroom until they discover which person matches each line on the sheet.

TIP #3: The Winning Equation

Game	☑ Opener	☐ Team-building
Categories:	☐ Energizer	☐ Review
	☐ Communication	☐ Topical:

■ **Purpose:** To help participants think creatively in any type of training class.

■ **Time Required:** 10 minutes.

■ **Size of Group:** Unlimited.

■ **Materials Required:** None.

■ **The Exercise in Action:** To help attendees begin thinking about creative solutions to problems, Gary Polain, vice president of business development with Priority Management in Bellevue, WA, poses the following brainteaser:

Polain writes the equation 5+5+5 = 550 on a flip chart at the front of the classroom. He then instructs trainees to copy the equation and to add one straight line to make it a correct statement. Polain tells participants that while adding a line through the equal sign to come up with 5+5+5 ≠ 550 is good thinking, it isn't the "right" answer he's looking for. See "Answer" graphic below for the solution.

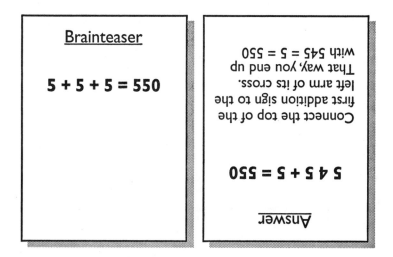

Brainteaser

5 + 5 + 5 = 550

Answer

5 4 5 + 5 = 550

Connect the top of the first addition sign to the left arm of its cross. That way, you end up with 545 = 5 = 550

Game Categories:	☐ Opener	☐ Team-building
	☐ Energizer	☑ Review
	☐ Communication	☐ Topical:

■ **Purpose:** To encourage participants to create their own review session and provide the trainer with a snapshot evaluation of the material.

■ **Time Required:** 15 minutes.

■ **Size of Group:** Unlimited.

■ **Materials Required:** None.

■ **The Exercise in Action:** At the end of a training program, have participants evaluate the curriculum by helping them create their own "fact/fiction" sheets. Individuals or small groups develop a series of true or false statements based on the information covered. Once the statements are written, participants exchange lists and then attempt to identify which statements are true and which are false. The exercise provides a thorough review and evaluation, and also can yield good questions for future tests.

Game Categories:	☐ Opener	☑ Team-building
	☐ Energizer	☐ Review
	☐ Communication	☐ Topical:

■ **Purpose:** To help teams learn to set — and meet — group goals.

■ **Time Required:** 30 minutes, stretched over the course of a one-day session or over two days in a longer class.

■ **Size of Group:** Unlimited, but trainees should work in teams of about four.

■ **Materials Required:** None.

■ **The Exercise in Action:** Faye Johnson, program specialist for the Bureau of Career Development, uses this technique to teach goal setting in teams:

Step 1: Ask participants to list the three most important "things" in their lives. Do not define "things." Have participants share what they've written in small groups and look for differences and common elements. Ask the group to consider whether the differences or similarities are affected by factors like age, job position, and upbringing.

Step 2: The next day (or later in the day if it's a one-day program) ask participants to imagine a stack of money — $30,000 or more — on the table in front of them. Ask them to list how they would spend the money and then share the lists with their small groups. Point out how some people make budget lists while others just get excited and buy, buy, buy. Then reflect on the items they have listed as important in the previous exercise and look for discrepancies. Use this as a time to let each person reevaluate what is really important.

Step 3: Ask participants to list 10 personal goals. They might include goals they have already achieved and goals not yet accomplished.

Step 4: Prioritize the goals list. Then list the roadblocks that have kept them from obtaining the top three goals. Ask a volunteer to share his or her top three goals and roadblocks.

Step 5: Have the group brainstorm to resolve problems or roadblocks. Demonstrate the group problem-solving technique and then stay clear of the process. Intervene only to keep the group on task, build network systems, ongoing analysis, and so on.

Once this technique has been modeled for one person, you can allow the small groups to spend time working through the process with each individual.

Game Categories:	□ Opener	□ Team-building
	□ Energizer	□ Review
	□ Communication	☑ Topical: Sales

■ **Purpose:** To help sales trainees more readily absorb product information, ultimately producing material that can be used in new sales trainee orientation, as review material, or as job aids.

■ **Time Required:** 10 to 15 minutes.

■ **Size of Group:** Unlimited.

■ **Materials Required:** None.

■ **The Exercise in Action:** Product knowledge information can be readily adapted to a "learn by doing" exercise. For instance, Martha Krzic, a training specialist in telemarketing with Xerox Canada, taps the experience of her sales training groups by asking them to brainstorm and list features and benefits of the products they sell, offer proof of those features and benefits, and put the items in descending order of importance.

After several groups have done this, she compiles the information and uses it as a product resource manual for all new representatives in the organization. With new products continually being introduced there is always a group working on a new "chapter." The exercise acts as a review for the groups, and their experience benefits the organization as it is passed on to others.

Similarly, Paula Peck, training officer at Union Safe Deposit Bank, uses small groups of four or fewer participants to create "features and benefits" charts for bank products. The charts include product names, features, benefits, target group, who handles the product, and any restrictions and/or requirements. Each group completes at least four charts and presents them to the entire training session. The entire group then discusses each chart. The charts can later be reduced or retyped on standard size paper and used as job aids when participants return to work.

Game	☐ **Opener**	☐ **Team-building**
Categories:	☑ **Energizer**	☐ **Review**
	☐ **Communication**	☐ **Topical:**

■ **Purpose:** To challenge participants to develop metaphors from everyday objects as an exercise in creativity.

■ **Time Required:** 10 to 20 minutes.

■ **Size of Group:** Unlimited, but participants should work in small groups of five to seven.

■ **Materials Required:** A paper sack for every small group filled with a variety of everyday objects.

■ **The Exercise in Action:** Alana Gallaher, a program specialist for the Department of Education in Tallahassee, FL, places a variety of objects in paper bags, such as a rubber band, paper clip, penny, eraser, pencil stub, or pen. She gives one sack to each small group and asks members of the group to choose an object out of the sack and find a way to relate the object to the training topic.

For example, a rubber band can be stretched — and a good instructor stretches the minds of his or her students; a paper clip holds things together — and a good manager communicates with the entire team in order to build team spirit and hold people together even in tough times.

TIP #8: A Matter of Taste

Game Categories:
☑ **Opener** ☐ **Team-building**
☐ **Energizer** ☐ **Review**
☐ **Communication** ☐ **Topical:**

■ **Purpose:** To introduce trainees to one another by uncovering their individual tastes.

■ **Time Required:** 10-25 minutes.

■ **Size of Group:** Unlimited.

■ **Materials Required:** None.

■ **The Exercise in Action:** Dave Dahlen, a park ranger with the National Park Service, helps participants get acquainted by asking a series of questions that reveal individual tastes and interests. For example,

"I enjoy...
    A. Classical
    B. Jazz
    C. Soul
    D. Rock
...music.

"Once each person has made a choice, participants divide into groups with similar musical tastes. After a short get-acquainted period, another question is asked, such as, "I enjoy Italian, Chinese, American, or French Cooking." The groups then change, based on those answers, and another short discussion period takes place.

TIP #9: The Name Game

Game Categories:
- ☐ Opener
- ☑ Energizer
- ☐ Communication
- ☑ Team-building
- ☐ Review
- ☐ Topical:

■ **Purpose:** To get small groups thinking together and creatively solving tough problems.

■ **Time Required:** 20 minutes.

■ **Size of Group:** Unlimited, but participants should work in small groups of five to seven.

■ **Materials Required:** A flip chart with the alphabet displayed vertically, prepared in advance by the trainer (see graphic).

■ **The Exercise in Action:**
After breaking the class into small groups Donna Adams, director of human resources for Miles Federal Credit Union, Elkhart, IN, displays a prepared flip-chart page with the alphabet written vertically on it. She then asks an attendee to share a random, sample sentence from a newspaper or other piece of written material and spells out that sentence vertically next to the alphabet, creating random pairs of letters, stopping the process when the 26th letter of the sentence matches the letter "z." (See example below, using the sentence "Now is the time for all good men to come to the aid of their country," ending on the "t" in the first "to.")

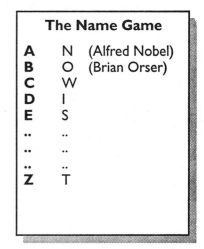

The Name Game		
A	N	(Alfred Nobel)
B	O	(Brian Orser)
C	W	
D	I	
E	S	
..	..	
..	..	
..	..	
Z	T	

The groups are then asked to come up with names of famous people or fictional characters that match the random initials — for example, AN = Alfred Nobel; BO = Brian Orser — using each set of letters once and only once. The team with the most names wins a small prize. (Note: This exercise is *not* as easy as it sounds.)

TIP #10: Old Dogs, New Tricks

Game Categories:

☐ **Opener**   ☐ **Team-building**
☐ **Energizer**   ☐ **Review**
☑ **Communication** ☐ **Topical:**

■ **Purpose:** To show participants that the rules of written language are constantly changing.

■ **Time Required:** 20 minutes.

■ **Size of Group:** Unlimited.

■ **Materials Required:** A selection of old books, either fiction or academic texts.

■ **The Exercise in Action:** People often regard the writing rules and styles they learn in high school or college as the final word on the topic and resist suggested changes. But written language, like spoken language, is in a constant state of flux, says Jane Watson, president of J. Watson & Associates, Toronto. People need to adapt their personal styles accordingly.

To make her point, Watson asks how many in her business communication courses have read *Anne of Green Gables* and enjoyed it. Several people usually raise their hands. She asks when they read it last. Most report it was years ago, during their childhoods. Most of the others have at least heard of the book.

Watson then reads the first page of the book aloud. Participants usually find it dull and uninteresting. Many are surprised at how stilted the writing seems. Next she reads the first few paragraphs from *A Child's Anne*, the same story updated for today's readers by Deirdre Kessler. Generally, all prefer the modern version.

To show that the lesson applies in the workplace, Watson reads selections from old grammar and style books — readily available in many used-book stores — and compares them against the latest editions. Everything from punctuation to the proper closing of a letter has changed with time.

The lesson gets people laughing and talking about changes they personally recall, Watson says, and opens participants' minds to the possibility that some of the guidelines they use in business correspondence may be outdated and in need of change.

TIP #11: How Much Is One Customer Worth?

Game Categories:
☐ Opener
☐ Energizer
☐ Communication
☐ Team-building
☐ Review
☑ Topical: Customer Service

■ **Purpose:** To quantify the need for a properly trained front-line staff.

■ **Time Required:** 10 minutes.

■ **Size of Group:** Unlimited.

■ **Materials Required:** A form similar to the graphic below, prepared in advance by the trainer.

■ **The Exercise in Action:** While few people will argue that having a properly trained front-line staff is critical to a business's success, it's an idea that is often hard to quantify. As a result, managers of front-line employees may not know just *how* financially damaging a single, poorly trained front-liner can be.

To illustrate the point, Rick Stamm, a partner with The Team Approach in Brownstown, PA, asks attendees of customer-service training sessions to complete the form below. He says he got the idea from the teachings of business consultant Tom Peters. "By the time people finish filling out the form," Stamm says, "they realize it makes a *lot* of financial sense to invest some time and money in making every employee a productive member of the customer service team."

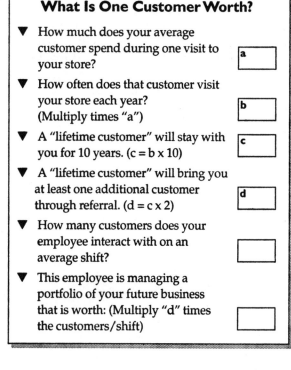

What Is One Customer Worth?

▼ How much does your average customer spend during one visit to your store? **a**

▼ How often does that customer visit your store each year? (Multiply times "a") **b**

▼ A "lifetime customer" will stay with you for 10 years. (c = b x 10) **c**

▼ A "lifetime customer" will bring you at least one additional customer through referral. (d = c x 2) **d**

▼ How many customers does your employee interact with on an average shift?

▼ This employee is managing a portfolio of your future business that is worth: (Multiply "d" times the customers/shift)

Game Categories:

☑ **Opener**   ☐ **Team-building**
☐ **Energizer**   ☐ **Review**
☐ **Communication**   ☐ **Topical:**

■ **Purpose:** To help participants recognize the innate ability they have to learn new material.

■ **Time Required:** 10 to 15 minutes.

■ **Size of Group:** Unlimited, but trainees should work in "rotating" pairs.

■ **Materials Required:** None.

■ **The Exercise in Action:** Carol Houseman, director of educational services for Mercy General Hospital, asks the class to form two concentric circles, with each person facing a partner. With the first partner they share their answers to this question: "What is a skill you learned as a child that you still do well?"

Once each partner has given an answer, the inner circle rotates one person clockwise, and the new partners discuss a second question: "What is a skill you learned as a child that you can't do well now?"

They rotate again and answer a third question: "Why did you retain that skill?"

They rotate to new partners once more and answer: "Why did you lose that skill?"

Finally, in small groups, ask participants to generate a series of learning points to help them retain the skills they learn from that particular class.

Game Categories:	☑ Opener	☐ Team-building
	☑ Energizer	☐ Review
	☐ Communication	☐ Topical:

■ **Purpose:** To demonstrate to trainees just how preconditioned the human animal tends to be.

■ **Time Required:** Five minutes.

■ **Size of Group:** Unlimited.

■ **Materials Required:** None.

■ **The Exercise in Action:** Ronald Rahn, a manager training specialist for the Lockheed Space Operations Co., secretly prints the words "red," "rose," and "chair" on a flip chart and covers them. He then tells participants he will ask them a series of questions and they should shout their answers. He says ,"Give me the name of a color, give me a name of a flower, and give me a name of a piece of furniture," and writes the response he most commonly hears on the flip chart.

When the hidden list is compared with the list made in class, he almost always has a complete match. Rahn uses this exercise as a springboard into a discussion of how conditioned people tend to be, and the importance of carefully examining our programming, so we are aware of choices we can make to consciously build new reactions and choices if needed.

The results are similar when he varies the exercise by giving each person an index card and asking them to quickly jot down the name of a color, flower, and piece of furniture. He then asks them to compare their answers in groups of five or six and discuss reasons for any similarities and differences.

Game	☐ Opener	☑ Team-building
Categories:	☐ Energizer	☐ Review
	☐ Communication	☐ Topical:

■ **Purpose:** To stress to teams the importance of achieving the right mix of team members' strengths and limitations to reach desired goals.

■ **Time Required:** 15 to 30 minutes.

■ **Size of Group:** Unlimited, but only nine participants can play at one time.

■ **Materials Required:** A long nylon rope. Nine blindfolds. A good-sized room, free of obstacles.

■ **The Exercise in Action:** Marilyn Russell, a nurse educator at the Dallas Medical Resource in Dallas, uses the "rope game" in team-building sessions:

Up to nine participants can play the game. A good-size room with all floor obstacles removed is needed. Participants are first asked to be blindfolded; if someone refuses he or she can assume an "observer" role in the game. Then a long nylon rope is tied end-to-end to make a continuous circle. Blindfolded participants are led to the rope and asked to grab it. The trainer then instructs the group to form a triangle with the nylon rope, or some other simple geometric figure. *It's important the trainer provide no other instructions.*

The group must then move together in a way that forms the geometric shape. Natural leaders and followers emerge as the group communicates and configures itself. When the group feels it's made the shape, trainees remove their blindfolds to see how well they have done as a group.

Next, blindfolds go back on as participants are instructed to make another shape. Those emerging as leaders in the first interaction are discreetly pulled aside by the trainer and told not to speak. Typically, that silence forces some of those who acted as followers in the first session to assume leadership roles.

Russell then debriefs, stressing that it is only the use of highly effective communication and cooperation that makes forming the shapes possible. "Any team's success depends upon how well each member uses his or her strengths and weaknesses to balance out the team's assets," she says. "A good team-building atmosphere stresses the importance of each member and increases everyone's self-esteem."

TIP #15: Sneaky Slogans

Game Categories:	☐ Opener	☐ Team-building
	☑ Energizer	☐ Review
	☐ Communication	☐ Topical:

■ **Purpose:** To actively break participants into pairs for small group activities.

■ **Time Required:** Five minutes.

■ **Size of Group:** Unlimited.

■ **Materials Required:** Index cards with slogans on them, prepared in advance by the trainer.

■ **The Exercise in Action:** Vickie Steffan, a trainer with Blue Cross Blue Shield of Virginia, Roanoke, VA, uses product/commercial slogans as a way to break a group into pairs for activities.

Steffan writes part of a commercial slogan on a card and puts the second half of the slogan on another card. For example, on card one she puts the famous Alka-Seltzer slogan, "Plop, plop, fizz, fizz..." and on card two, "Oh, what a relief it is." She hands out the cards and asks participants to find their partners.

Game Categories:	☐ Opener	☑ Team-building
	☐ Energizer	☐ Review
	☐ Communication	☑ Topical: Diversity

■ **Purpose:** To combine a team-building exercise with a lesson in diversity by having teams share information about themselves with others in the group.

■ **Time Required:** 15 to 25 minutes.

■ **Size of Group:** Unlimited, but trainees should work in small groups of four to six.

■ **Materials Required:** A sheet of questions, prepared in advance by the trainer. Post-It Notes.

■ **The Exercise in Action:** Susan Partee, a training assistant with O'Reilly Automotive Inc., Springfield, MO, creates a list of questions like those shown in the example below — interesting, but not embarrassing — being careful to have at least as many questions as there are members on the largest team.

Partee then breaks the class into small groups of four to six trainees and hands out copies to each participant, asking them to cross off those questions that exceed the number of group members. For example, a team of six would answer only the first six questions. (Flip-chart pages, each bearing one question, are posted on the wall for later use.)

Partee instructs participants to label question number one with the name of the person directly to their left, number two with the next person, and so on around the table until each question has a member's name beside it. The result: Each person's name should appear beside a given question on only one other person's sheet.

Next she gives participants Post-It Notes and instructs them to ask the person whose names appear next to each question on their sheets for the corresponding answers. Answers are recorded (along with the respondent's name) on the Post-It Notes and placed on the appropriate flip-chart page.

When everyone is finished, Partee reads as many of the answers as time allows. In the discussion that follows, Partee asks participants what they have learned about their teammates that might contribute to their groups' success.

TIP #17: Role Reversal

Game Categories:	☐ Opener	☐ Team-building
	☐ Energizer	☐ Review
	☑ Communication	☑ Topical: Conflict Resolution

■ **Purpose:** To illustrate more constructive ways to solve conflict.

■ **Time Required:** 10 to 20 minutes.

■ **Size of Group:** Unlimited.

■ **Materials Required:** None.

■ **The Exercise in Action:** In workshops composed of both supervisors and subordinates, Larry Julian, manager of employee involvement at the Philip Morris Manufacturing Center, Richmond, VA, finds one of the group's favorite pastimes is finger-pointing. And the finger most often points toward management as the words "they" and "them" become a part of group vocabulary, he says.

But now, when employees begin to point fingers and place blame, Julian attempts to intervene using role-plays. He first places a chair behind a desk or table along with a name tent that says "The Boss." He asks the finger-pointing employee to take a seat behind the table in The Boss's chair, and asks another employee — preferably a supervisor — to take a seat in a chair in front of the table and assume the role of the finger-pointing employee. The finger-pointer then presents the problem to The Boss. The Boss is asked to form a solution to the problem from a supervisor's point of view.

Obviously, excellent facilitation skills are needed in the role-plays to prevent confrontations. But Julian's experience has been that placing the finger-pointer in his or her new role provides a new perspective on the "need for people to become part of the solution rather than part of the problem."

TIP #18: True Confession Toothpicks

Game Categories:	☑ Opener	☐ Team-building
	☑ Energizer	☐ Review
	☐ Communication	☐ Topical:

■ **Purpose:** To challenge participants to think creatively.

■ **Time Required:** 15 minutes.

■ **Size of Group:** Unlimited.

■ **Materials Required:** A large supply of toothpicks.

■ **The Exercise in Action:** Participants are challenged to think creatively, and also to make "true confessions" during this opener recommended by Lori Preston, training specialist at Electronic Data Systems.

Start by giving each participant 10 toothpicks or other counters. Then ask the first participant to talk about something they have never done, for example, "I've never jaywalked." After the statement anyone in the group who has jaywalked has to forfeit a toothpick to the kitty. Then the next person shares one thing he or she has never done, and again anyone who has done it loses a toothpick. The disclosures continue around the room until someone has lost all 10 toothpicks. It's an entertaining way for people to get to know one another both by the things they have done, and the things they haven't done.

TIP #19: Personal Introductions

Game Categories:	☑ Opener	☐ Team-building
	☐ Energizer	☐ Review
	☐ Communication	☐ Topical:

■ **Purpose:** To introduce participants to one another in a training session.

■ **Time Required:** 10 minutes.

■ **Size of Group:** Unlimited, but participants should work in small groups of five or six.

■ **Materials Required:** Several small paper bags.

■ **The Exercise in Action:** Nina Policastro, training director for the Junior League in Dix Hills, NY, gives each participant a small paper bag and then asks them to put three items from their wallet, briefcase, or purse inside the bag that show something about their personality or life-style. In small groups of five or six, people then share why they selected the items.

To make this opener more program-oriented, ask people to select three items that make statements about their jobs. If they're in customer service, for instance, ask them to select something that relates to how they help customers.

TIP #20: Baby Pictures

Game Categories:	☑ Opener	☐ Team-building
	☐ Energizer	☐ Review
	☐ Communication	☑ Topical: Change Management

■ **Purpose:** To creatively introduce to one another before a session and make a learning point as well.

■ **Time Required:** 20 minutes.

■ **Size of Group:** Unlimited.

■ **Materials Required:** Baby photos of participants, sent to the trainer in advance of the session.

■ **The Exercise in Action:** Using participants' baby photos can help break the ice and drive home some learning points, according to Lisa Monopoli of National Car Rental System. She has participants attempt to send a baby photo to her prior to the seminar. She numbers and displays the baby pictures, and has participants match them up by voting on who's who. When the votes are tallied everyone has a good laugh, she says. Monopoli says this activity is especially effective for seminars that include a combination of work peers of different professional levels.

Monopoli says that aside from being fun, the opener helps make two learning points:

▼ When conducting a class with participants who are of different professional levels, the activity helps break the ice by pointing out that we all started out on the same level (at about six to nine pounds).

▼ When conducting courses where change is the focus, it helps to demonstrate how much change each of us has already been through and that change is inevitable.

Game Categories:	☐ Opener	☑ Team-building
	☑ Energizer	☑ Review
	☐ Communication	☐ Topical:

■ **Purpose:** To lead attendees through a creative review session.

■ **Time Required:** 30 minutes.

■ **Size of Group:** Unlimited.

■ **Materials Required:** Any props that may help convert the classroom to a ballpark (for example, plastic bats, baseball caps, etc.)

■ **The Exercise in Action:** Participants in training at Great Plains Software in Fargo, ND, are told to arrive wearing a uniform and sneakers and to be prepared to "play ball" during review sessions.

Internal product trainer Jeanne Rodenbiker quickly converts her training room into a playing field, using chairs as bases, giving baseball hats to trainees, and keeping an inflatable bat on hand to add a little ballpark flavor. She divides the class into groups and has them choose their own names, usually something related to the topic.

When the first team comes up to bat, one player draws a baseball card from a hat. Each card is marked as a single, double, triple, or home run. The pitcher (instructor) relays a question of the appropriate level of difficulty (for example, triples are more difficult than doubles.) Although only one team member advances the indicated bases, the entire team can discuss the question before answering. This eliminates putting students on the spot and encourages group interaction. If answers require visual aids, the team uses a whiteboard to diagram its responses.

The instructor serves as pitcher and umpire, providing hints or designating time limits as to when questions must be answered. After three outs (misses), the second team bats.

Rodenbiker says the energy level in this exercise is usually high and teams become quite competitive. She has had teams develop cheers and a few enthusiastic players even slide into bases. In most courses, she fits in the "game innings" after completing major sections of the material.

TIP #22: Body Parts

Game Categories:	☐ Opener	☑ Team-building
	☐ Energizer	☐ Review
	☐ Communication	☐ Topical:

■ **Purpose:** To help participants learn to work as a team.

■ **Time Required:** 10 to 15 minutes.

■ **Size of Group:** Unlimited.

■ **Materials Required:** Cards with the name of a body part written on them, prepared in advance by the trainer.

■ **The Exercise in Action:** Janet Bradly, human resource consultant with Work Cover, emphasizes working as a team, a body, or a group with this exercise:

Bradly gives each individual a card indicating what part of the body they are to represent: right leg, left leg, right arm, eyes, nose, etc. Then without speaking, they have to find the other people who are the same body part. Once that is accomplished they move to step three — finding enough people to form a complete body, again without speaking.

Finally the body is whole and learns to walk, run, breathe, etc., and demonstrates the ability to do those tasks.

**Game
Categories:**

☐ Opener
☑ Energizer
☐ Communication

☐ Team-building
☐ Review
☐ Topical:

■ **Purpose:** To divide participants into small groups.

■ **Time Required:** Five minutes.

■ **Size of Group:** Unlimited.

■ **Materials Required:** A deck of playing cards.

■ **The Exercise in Action:** Here are two ideas for creatively dividing participants into small groups:

▼ *Use ordinary playing cards.* If you've got 32 participants, for example, and you want them in four groups of eight, simply take eight spades, eight diamonds, and so on out of the deck. Shuffle, distribute the cards, and then assemble groups according to suit. The same can be done more humorously using children's card decks, such as Crazy Eights. Form your groups based upon identical pictures in the deck.

▼ *Use the experience levels that exist in the group.* Divide your participants into two groups and have one form a circle facing inward, the other form a circle inside the first circle facing outward so each person looks at a partner. Tell the outer group to move clockwise and the inner group to move counterclockwise until you tell them to stop. Have the people directly facing each other spend a few minutes talking about their previous jobs and how those positions prepared them for their current positions. That information is then used for everyone to introduce their partners to the rest of the group. Clusters of partners can form the work groups for the next part of the class.

TIP #24: Tag Team Role-Plays

Game Categories:	☐ Opener	☑ Team-building
	☐ Energizer	☐ Review
	☐ Communication	☐ Topical:

■ **Purpose:** To introduce a sense of teamwork into role-plays.

■ **Time Required:** 10 to 20 minutes.

■ **Size of Group:** 10 to 18.

■ **Materials Required:** None.

■ **The Exercise in Action:** A different twist on role-plays is guaranteed to keep participants attentive and build a team atmosphere, according to Shirley Poertner, staff consultant for training and development, Meredith Corp. Rather than using traditional role-plays for senior-level managers, Poertner uses a "tag-team" approach.

She divides the managers into two groups of five participants each. Group A members are all given the first half of a role-play to read, and Group B members are given the other half of the same role-play. One manager from each group sits at a desk or table and begins the role-play, with the other four managers from each group lined up behind that person.

At any point, the manager from either team in the role-play can reach behind and touch or "tag" any of the other managers who are standing behind them. At that point, the tagged team member steps forward and continues the role-play.

Poertner says the exercise is effective because all participants need to stay attentive so they're prepared to jump in.

A variation on this is for the waiting team members to take the initiative in tagging their way into the role-play.

TIP #25: Word Games

Game   ☐ Opener   ☐ Team-building
Categories: ☐ Energizer   ☑ Review
             ☐ Communication   ☐ Topical:

■ **Purpose:** To lead participants through a review game.

■ **Time Required:** 10 to 20 minutes.

■ **Size of Group:** Unlimited.

■ **Materials Required:** None.

■ **The Exercise in Action:** Loretta Gutting, manager of Southwestern Bell in St. Louis, uses a variation of the board game, Scrabble, as a review exercise. Gutting writes one word in the center of a piece of graph flip-chart paper. Students must build on that word and subsequent words in a Scrabble or crossword puzzle fashion. Students can use any letters to build words. Gutting says it's proven to be a great way to review or brainstorm topics.

Using a variation on the word game, Scrabble, is an effective way to review or brainstorm topics.

TIP #26: Sea If Ewe Can Find the Errers

Game Categories:

- ☐ Opener
- ☑ Energizer
- ☐ Communication
- ☐ Team-building
- ☐ Review
- ☑ Topical: Conflict Management

■ **Purpose:** To provide an exercise that challenges participants to think creatively.

■ **Time Required:** 10 minutes.

■ **Size of Group:** Unlimited.

■ **Materials Required:** None.

■ **The Exercise in Action:** For a smooth transition after a break, write this statement on a flip chart or transparency during the break so participants can work on it when they return to the room. Allow people to work individually or in groups to find the errors:

> "You may not belief that there are six errers in this short paragraph. Studi the paragraph carefuly. You can reed it as many times as necessary. Don't give up too easily. See if you can find all of them."

Most participants will find five but few will ever find the sixth. The sixth is simply that there are only five errors (so it's an error to say there are six). The exercise points out how we often think inflexibly and fail to consider all the options when problem solving.

TIP #27: Connect the Dots

Game Categories:	☑ Opener	☐ Team-building
	☑ Energizer	☐ Review
	☐ Communication	☐ Topical:

■ **Purpose:** To provide an exercise that challenges participants to think creatively.

■ **Time Required:** 10 minutes.

■ **Size of Group:** Unlimited.

■ **Materials Required:** None.

■ **The Exercise in Action:** To show his trainees the importance of an open mind, creativity, and problem solving, Jack McKown, process controller for Hallmark Cards in Kansas City, MO, uses a "connect the dots" exercise as a brainteaser opener.

Draw a dot pattern (shown below) on a sheet of paper (make dots at least 1/4 inch diameter). Then tell participants that if they are creative, they can draw a line through all the dots with only one line. The only rule is that the lines must be drawn straight.

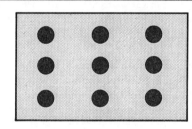

To set up the brainteaser: Give each participant a sheet of paper with nine evenly spaced dots on it. Tell participants the objective of the exercise is to connect all the dots with only one line.

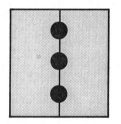

Solution: Fold the paper over onto itself toward the center (so one-half of each dot from the left side of the sheet connects with one-half of each dot from the right side). Then draw a line down through the aligned dots.

Game Categories:	☑ Opener	☐ Team-building
	☐ Energizer	☐ Review
	☐ Communication	☐ Topical:

■ **Purpose:** To satisfy participants' curiosity about their classmates' tenure with the company.

■ **Time Required:** 10 minutes.

■ **Size of Group:** Unlimited.

■ **Materials Required:** None.

■ **The Exercise in Action:** Most participants are naturally curious about how much experience others in a class have with their companies. Liz Seely, a market support sales trainer for MCI, starts her sessions by asking participants to write their guesses of the average tenure of all participants. Then she asks each table to add up their number of years with the company and uses that number to find her average for the room. The person with the closest guess wins a small prize.

Depending on the amount of experience represented within the class, Seely makes a point about the incredible amount of experience a group can bring to a class, and that participants shouldn't be afraid to ask peers for help when they need it.

TIP #29: Pennies Puzzler

Game Categories:	☐ Opener	☐ Team-building
	☑ Energizer	☐ Review
	☐ Communication	☐ Topical:

■ **Purpose:** To stress creativity and get participants to "think outside the box."

■ **Time Required:** 10 to 15 minutes.

■ **Size of Group:** 10 to 15.

■ **Materials Required:** 12 pennies per attendee.

■ **The Exercise in Action:** Cindy Forbes, assistant vice president of MBNA America in Newark, DE, gives each training participant 12 pennies and asks them to form a square with five pennies on each side. After giving trainees an appropriate amount of time to solve the puzzler, she explains the solution (see below).

When the solution is explained, Forbes says, it helps participants realize their thinking was unnecessarily restrictive. She then begins a discussion on the benefit of finding creative solutions to problems.

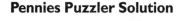

Pennies Puzzler Solution

Here's the solution: Stack two pennies on top of each other for each of the four corners, then place one penny between each corner to form a square.

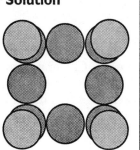

TIP #30: Killing Close-ended Questions

Game Categories:	☑ Opener	☐ Team-building
	☐ Energizer	☐ Review
	☑ Communication	☐ Topical:

■ **Purpose:** To quickly and graphically demonstrate the limitations of closed-ended questions.

■ **Time Required:** 15 minutes.

■ **Size of Group:** Unlimited.

■ **Materials Required:** A list of characters, prepared in advance by the trainer. Name tags.

■ **The Exercise in Action:** Many types of training emphasize the importance of asking cogent questions to elicit the kind of information you are seeking from others. Cheryl Carter, an employee relations specialist at Philip Morris U.S.A., uses the following exercise to demonstrate the limitations of closed-ended questions.

Carter develops a list of characters based on popular figures as diverse as Woody Woodpecker, John F. Kennedy, and Cinderella. She writes one name per name tag, enough for the class.

She then places a tag on each participant's back, and allows participants five to seven minutes to find out what their new identity is. The ground rules:

1. You can only ask questions that require a yes or no answer.
2. You must ask at least five different people a different question.

Once time is up, Carter reconvenes the group, discovers who has guessed correctly, and has participants share what types of questions they used to arrive at that information.

Game Categories:	☐ Opener	☐ Team-building
	☐ Energizer	☑ Review
	☐ Communication	☐ Topical:

■ **Purpose:** To help attendees review technical material, especially many steps in a process.

■ **Time Required:** 15 to 25 minutes.

■ **Size of Group:** Unlimited, but trainees should work in small groups of three to six.

■ **Materials Required:** A poster-size diagram of the various steps of the process being reviewed, Post-It Notes numbered to correspond to the number of parts, and a numbered list of the descriptions of each part's function.

■ **The Exercise in Action:** "Name That Part" is an exercise specifically designed to review a technical diagram for a truck air brake system, but Carol Young, project coordinator for SUNY Empire State College, believes the tactic could be used in any training of a detailed piece of equipment or a lengthy process.

The class first reviews the diagram and functions of each part. Next, the class is divided into groups and each group is given a poster/diagram, Post-Its, and the list of functions. The groups are allowed five minutes to label each part with the numbered Post-Its corresponding to the function. Then each group moves to the next table to check that group's diagram, while Young shows the correct answers on a transparency.

The posters can later be hung in the participants' workplaces as job aids.

TIP #32: Playing the Numbers

Game Categories:	☐ Opener ☑ Energizer ☐ Communication	☐ Team-building ☐ Review ☐ Topical:

■ **Purpose:** To engage attendees in a creative exercise after a break or lunch.

■ **Time Required:** 10 minutes.

■ **Size of Group:** Unlimited.

■ **Materials Required:** None.

■ **The Exercise in Action:** Here's a quick exercise you can use after lunch or a break. Place these numbers on a flip chart or whiteboard:

8, 11, 15, 5, 14, 1, 7, 6, 10, 13, 3, 12, 2

Tell the audience, "You're seeing all the numbers from one to 15 with the exception of four and nine. Your task is to decide why the numbers are arranged in this sequence, then put the missing numbers in their proper places."

Take the test yourself right now. After you've made your decision, turn this page upside down for the correct answer.

8, 11, 15, 5, 4, 14, 9, 1, 7, 6, 10, 13, 3, 12, 2

Answer: The numbers are listed alphabetically. Therefore, four goes after five and nine follows 14.

TIP #33: On the Other Hand...

Game	☐ Opener	☐ Team-building
Categories:	☐ Energizer	☐ Review
	☐ Communication	☑ Topical: Orientation

■ **Purpose:** To show new employees how unfamiliarity with a task or job can be overcome.

■ **Time Required:** 10 to 15 minutes.

■ **Size of Group:** Unlimited.

■ **Materials Required:** Writing materials for each participant.

■ **The Exercise in Action:** Susan Boyd, director of corporate support and development at PC Concepts, Wayne, PA, asks participants to write a word related to the course topic. She times one person to see how long the task takes.

She asks participants to switch to their other hand and write the word again. Boyd times the same person to get a comparative example. Boyd observes the following reactions: expressions such as, "You've got to be kidding!" Participant reactions include nervous laughter, hesitance to start, reluctance to try, attempts to write with the other hand then switching back to their writing hand, deeper concentration, and closely watching the pen and the word being formed.

Talk about the results. Typically writing the word takes about four to six seconds the first time, and about twice as long with the other hand. Boyd asks the class why it took so long the second time.

Analyze the quality of the second writing sample. Obviously, it will look worse than the first sample.

Relate the exercise to learning. Boyd tells the class that if they lost the use of their writing hand, what they just experienced would happen over the first two or three weeks as they started to learn how to write with their other hand. By the fourth week, they would see improvement in the time and quality of their writing. By the end of four to six months, they would have assimilated the new skill.

In conclusion, Boyd tells attendees that the next two or three weeks will be the hardest, because doing tasks with a new technique will seem to take more time, require more effort, and still may not meet their quality standards. She encourages them to hang in there, because once they get past the three-week hurdle, they will see a tremendous improvement in both time and quality as the new learning is assimilated into their daily routines.

Game Categories:	□ Opener	□ Team-building
	☑ Energizer	□ Review
	□ Communication	☑ Topical: Customer Service

■ **Purpose:** To sensitize customer service trainees to customer needs.

■ **Time Required:** 20 minutes.

■ **Size of Group:** Eight to 12.

■ **Materials Required:** A "registration" form, prepared in advance.

■ **The Exercise in Action:** Are your customer service employees insensitive to customer needs, despite extensive training? If so, this empathy-raising "registration" exercise used by Susan Glasstetter of Indiana Hospital will motivate them to walk for a few minutes in the other person's moccasins.

Glasstetter developed a one-page form that trainees are required to complete to register officially for a customer service training program. The questions are related to education and personnel policies and are slanted so that only recent high school or college graduates, education specialists, or human resource personnel could possibly provide immediate, accurate answers. Glasstetter's role is to register each applicant in as detached, professional, and vaguely impatient a manner as possible.

She reports reactions to this little exercise as very enlightening. "It is difficult to maintain my role while listening to comments such as, 'I don't remember what my high school Scholastic Aptitude Test (SAT) scores were! Why do you need that?' and 'What do you mean by employee number? I didn't even know I *had* a number!'"

After the forms are completed and the group is seated, Glasstetter asks participants to comment on the registration process. In general, they don't like it. Before they begin complaining again, she asks if their experience helped them see how customers may be confused about company policies that the trainees find commonplace. For a minute there is silence. As the light dawns, heads begin to nod in agreement and some complaints continue about the exercise "not being fair."

The empathy-raising exercise has obvious benefits: Employees can truly experience the viewpoint of their customers. It can also have one serious drawback, depending on your group: Those who are neither ready nor willing to admit they need a change of attitude may resent having their eyes opened.

Game	❐ **Opener**	❐ **Team-building**
Categories:	❐ **Energizer**	☑ **Review**
	❐ **Communication**	❐ **Topical:**

■ **Purpose:** To keep important course material fresh in attendees' minds once they're back on the job.

■ **Time Required:** 10 minutes.

■ **Size of Group:** Unlimited.

■ **Materials Required:** A "Question of the Week," prepared in advance by the trainer.

■ **The Exercise in Action:** To improve comprehension and retention once class is over, Heidi Marker, a trainer for a full-service resort hotel in Lancaster, PA, puts a "Question of the Week" poster on an employee bulletin board. Each week she posts a question relating to a work topic on a sheet of paper with the answer hidden underneath.

Marker says employees from other departments stop by to flip through the pages, and managers use the board to relay information.

Game Categories:	☑ **Opener**	☑ **Team-building**
	☐ **Energizer**	☐ **Review**
	☐ **Communication**	☐ **Topical:**

■ **Purpose:** To open a course by putting in attendees' hands some of the items they'll use during the session.

■ **Time Required:** 15 minutes.

■ **Size of Group:** Unlimited.

■ **Materials Required:** Stickers with letters on them. A variety of items trainees typically use in class (for example, markers, handouts, etc.).

■ **The Exercise in Action:** Mandy Proctor, a nurse educator for Sinai Samaritan Medical Center in Milwaukee, starts some of her classes by sending participants on a scavenger hunt that she sets up in the training room. She places letter stickers above the items and as the participants find each item, they remove the letters and place them on their instruction sheets.

When the participants are finished, the letters spell out the words "Welcome to 5A (Proctor's unit). We're glad you're here."

The items you list for the hunt could be items participants will use during the training programs such as flip charts, markers, and other supplies, or the pieces of equipment they're going to learn about.

Game Categories:	☐ Opener	☑ Team-building
	☐ Energizer	☐ Review
	☐ Communication	☐ Topical:

■ **Purpose:** To illustrate the importance of cooperation and teamwork.

■ **Time Required:** 10 minutes.

■ **Size of Group:** Unlimited.

■ **Materials Required:** None.

■ **The Exercise in Action:** Helen Molnar, consultant for the Public Service Board in Melbourne, Australia, has participants play this game to help build team work: Participants stand face-to-face in pairs, holding each other's right hands as if they were going to shake hands. The aim of the game is for each individual to score as many points as possible in 30 seconds. Participants score by touching their right hip with their right hand while still holding their partner's hand. Each touch equals one point.

When time is up, Molnar has participants stand and tell their scores, then sit down whenever a score higher than their own is reported. At the end, the most "cooperative" team is standing. Frequently, people will try to pull their partner's hand, scoring as few as four to six points. Working together, others may score as many as 100 points.

TIP #38: 30 Seconds

Game Categories:

☐ Opener   ☐ Team-building
☑ Energizer   ☐ Review
☐ Communication   ☐ Topical:

■ **Purpose:** To quickly energize and challenge participants.

■ **Time Required:** 30 seconds.

■ **Size of Group:** Unlimited.

■ **Materials Required:** None.

■ **The Exercise in Action:** Trainer Gerri Borden of Troy Savings, uses 30-second games to energize participants throughout sessions. Borden chooses a topic and challenges participants to list as many titles as they can from the category, such as "professional football" or "basketball teams" or "Disney movies." When the 30 seconds are up, participants show how many items they have listed. Borden writes the number after their names on a flip chart.

Borden uses this activity before each break and at the end of the day, but is careful to use a variety of categories, for example, things used in cooking, fruits, vegetables, musical instruments, birds, types of clouds, etc. She awards a prize to the person with the highest total.

TIP #39: Elevator Speech

Game Categories:	☐ Opener	☐ Team-building
	☐ Energizer	☐ Review
	☑ Communication	☑ Topical: Train-the-Trainer

■ **Purpose:** To help trainers — especially new trainers — better monitor time in the classroom and answer participant questions with greater brevity.

■ **Time Required:** 20 to 30 minutes.

■ **Size of Group:** Eight to 12.

■ **Materials Required:** Prepared questions, written in advance by the trainer on index cards.

■ **The Exercise in Action:** Linda Shear, a professional development manager with Lotus Development Corp. in San Francisco, uses these two exercises to make points in her train-the-trainer classes:

▼ *Time control:* Ask participants to close their eyes and raise their hands when they think 30 seconds has elapsed, opening their eyes as they put up their hands. Using a stop watch, the trainer raises her own hand to mark the 30-second interval, and records times as participant hands go up.

One telling result, Shear says, is, "Trainers who tend to ramble a lot and whose training programs consistently go over the allotted time are the same people who raise their hands far after the 30 seconds is past." Trainers who tend to barely finish their sessions in time usually raise their hands a little before the 30 seconds. The exercise helps trainers understand their own views of time, and "whether they have a tendency to think time goes slowly and therefore think they have a lot of it, or that it passes quickly and they need to rush," she says.

▼ *Giving concise answers:* Shear uses an "elevator speech" analogy to help trainers develop skills to answer trainees' questions concisely: Imagine you just stepped into an elevator, and your boss's boss gets on and asks a question. You want to make a good impression, but only have 20 seconds to answer before she leaves the elevator.

Shear has trainer candidates go through the scenario one by one. She also has each participant stand in front of the room and answer questions other participants have asked and that she has written on index cards. Participants have 20 seconds to answer, thinking "elevator" all the while.

TIP #40: The Envelope, Please

Game Categories:
- ☐ Opener
- ☐ Energizer
- ☐ Communication
- ☐ Team-building
- ☐ Review
- ☑ Topical: Management

■ **Purpose:** To show new managers the importance of immediately documenting information that requires accurate reporting — for conducting performance appraisals, for instance.

■ **Time Required:** 10 to 15 minutes.

■ **Size of Group:** Unlimited.

■ **Materials Required:** Photocopies of scenic photographs. Envelopes.

■ **The Exercise in Action:** Pam Meier, a training and development consultant for the Dayton Hudson Co., Minneapolis, MN, hands out photocopies of scenic photographs — usually street scenes with people and lots of detail. She asks participants to study the pictures for one minute and then fold them up and seal them in envelopes. Later, after a break, she asks them to write what they remember about the pictures.

Their answers are then folded and paper-clipped to the envelope. Later in the day, when the topic of documentation comes up, she asks them to pass their sealed envelopes to another person at their tables (based on the number of people per table, she has a different scene for each person). That person reads the description and tries to imagine what the scene looks like and writes a brief description. They finally open the envelope to compare how closely the picture they've developed in their minds matches the original scene.

The learning point: Memory, recall, and attention to detail are important, but immediately documenting specifics is more important when accuracy is essential.

Game   ☑ **Opener**   ☐ **Team-building**
Categories: ☐ **Energizer**   ☐ **Review**
               ☐ **Communication**   ☐ **Topical:**

■ **Purpose:** To symbolically rid participants of their greatest "learning fear."

■ **Time Required:** Five minutes.

■ **Size of Group:** Unlimited.

■ **Materials Required:** A supply of magician's "flash paper," available at most magic shops.

■ **The Exercise in Action:** As participants enter Gary Weaver's training room, each is given a small piece of magician's flash paper (about 2 inches square). He doesn't tell them the purpose of the paper, nor that it's "trick" material. He also places a lit candle at the front of the room.

Weaver, an industry trainer with Canadian Valley Vo-Tech in El Reno, OK, asks participants to write their biggest learning obstacle or fear on the paper — speaking up in class, for example. They then walk up, one by one, to the front of the room, share the concern or fear with the rest of the class, and ignite the flash paper in the candle by tossing it — safely away from others — in the air toward the candle, where it burns quickly before coming down.

Weaver says the symbolism isn't lost on trainees, who are comforted hearing others reveal fears of their own. "It's a great way to watch learning obstacles 'go up in smoke' before the training begins," he says.

TIP #42: A Cup of Group Cheer

Game	☐ Opener	☑ Team-building
Categories:	☑ Energizer	☐ Review
	☐ Communication	☐ Topical:

■ **Purpose:** To promote cross-company and interdepartmental collaboration and partnering.

■ **Time Required:** 10 minutes.

■ **Size of Group:** Unlimited.

■ **Materials Required:** None.

■ **The Exercise in Action:** Irene Ward, president of Irene Ward & Associates, Columbus, OH, helps participants of a one-day team-building seminar foster a true sense of teamwork by asking pre-assigned small groups to develop a team cheer.

They are given about five minutes to do so, Ward says, before sharing the cheer with the entire group. Then, for the remainder of the day, each time the various teams complete a problem-solving assignment and prior to reporting to the entire class, they are asked to do their group cheer to celebrate the victory (usually about three or four times per day, Ward says).

She also asks the groups to do their cheers right after lunch to demonstrate how much the energy level has dropped since the morning session. "It gets everyone laughing at how pitiful the various team cheers sound," Ward says, and the strategy helps heighten awareness about staying alert after lunch.

TIP #43: Pass the Hat

Game Categories:
- ☐ Opener
- ☐ Energizer
- ☐ Communication
- ☐ Team-building
- ☑ Review
- ☐ Topical:

■ **Purpose:** To give participants a more active role in review sessions.

■ **Time Required:** 10-15 minutes.

■ **Size of Group:** Unlimited.

■ **Materials Required:** Writing materials for everyone. A small hat or basket.

■ **The Exercise in Action:** Aline Hurst, a training officer at First Security Bank of Idaho, Boise, has participants create as well as answer a variety of review questions by asking them to write review questions every so often and drop them in a hat or basket she brings around the room.

Hurst also places some of her own questions in the hat, usually not related to course content and more personal in nature, like "What is the accomplishment you are most proud of?"

Throughout the session Hurst passes the hat and asks participants to pull out and answer a question. Because participants don't know what kind of questions they'll get, it forces them to pay a little closer attention in class. And Hurst says the technique "keeps things more interesting while reinforcing concepts."

TIP #44: Just-in-Time Review

Game Categories:	☐ Opener	☐ Team-building
	☑ Energizer	☑ Review
	☐ Communication	☐ Topical:

■ **Purpose:** To set up a review session before class even begins.

■ **Time Required:** 10 minutes.

■ **Size of Group:** Unlimited.

■ **Materials Required:** Questions on index cards, prepared in advance by the trainer.

■ **The Exercise in Action:** Setting up your review sessions *before* a course begins is a great way to keep energy levels up and avoid the trap of announcing, "Let's review." Done well, this technique may not even be recognized by participants as a review tool:

Nancy Hall, a trainer in Winston-Salem, NC, prepares a number of index cards with questions on them and distributes them at the beginning of the session. The cards are numbered, and the questions — while pertinent to the course material — are generally opinion-oriented, such as, "What traits would an ideal supervisor possess?" Then, just before relevant material is covered, Hall reads a number and the participant with the corresponding card reads the question and answers it.

Creative twists can turn Hall's exercise into a small-group energizer. When a number is called, for example, the instructor may opt to have that participant's small group (instead of the individual) answer within 90 seconds.

TIP #45: Optical Illusions

Game Categories:	☐ Opener	☐ Team-building
	☑ Energizer	☐ Review
	☐ Communication	☐ Topical:

■ **Purpose:** To demonstrate that things aren't always as they seem in everyday encounters with others.

■ **Time Required:** 15 minutes.

■ **Size of Group:** Unlimited.

■ **Materials Required:** A series of optical illusions suggested in part by the book, *Experimenting with Illusions*, by Robert Gardner (Franklin Watts, 800-621-1115), which contains a variety of noncopyrighted illusions with lines, 3-D illusions, and magic tricks.

■ **The Exercise in Action:** The human mind is trained to draw conclusions based on what it *thinks* the eyes see, says Bill Lange, a training specialist at Bank One Columbus, Westerville, OH. But judging anything — people in particular — based on visual input alone can lead to misguided conclusions.

Lange demonstrates by displaying a series of optical illusions, one at a time. He asks the class to discuss what they think they see before moving on to the next one. He doesn't offer any explanations until he has shown the entire set. When he's been through the pictures once, he shows each one again, and explains the trick it plays on the eye.

Lange then ties the lesson to real life: We often judge people based on first impressions. If they appear unkempt, we may assume they're poor or unintelligent. If they grow verbally hostile we may assume they're irrational or belligerent by nature. Conversely, if they dress well, we may conclude they are well-mannered or honest. All these presumptions can be wrong.

Lange asks students to offer possible explanations for any of the above sorts of people not meeting first expectations. A disheveled person, for example, may have come in from bad weather; a person who seems inordinately angry may have had a bad experience prior to your encounter.

The lesson is a classic: Don't judge a book by its cover.

TIP #46: You Bet Your Life

Game Categories:	☑ Opener	☐ Team-building
	☐ Energizer	☐ Review
	☐ Communication	☐ Topical:

■ **Purpose:** To use a variation of a familiar game to break the ice in a session.

■ **Time Required:** 30 minutes.

■ **Size of Group:** 12 to 15

■ **Materials Required:** Poker chips with "secret" words written on them, prepared in advance by the trainer.

■ **The Exercise in Action:** Linda Williams a senior education and development specialist with First Trust Corp. in Denver, uses this opener modeled on the old Groucho Marx TV show, *You Bet Your Life*.

As participants enter the room, she gives each a poker chip with a "secret" word written on it and asks them not to share it with anyone. Once the whole group has gathered, she explains the object of the activity is to meet as many people as possible. The incentive to do that is a prize awarded to the person who collects the most secret words.

To collect a word, a participant must say the word in normal conversation with the person who holds it. When the word is said, the owner of the secret word fesses up and shows the other person the poker chip with word on it. Each person keeps track of his or her score. Williams chooses words with a high probability of being part of a "getting to know you" conversation. The secret words remain active throughout the activity, so participants can run up a large score.

Other guidelines include:

▼ In group discussions, the poker chips should be shown only to the individual who says the secret word.

▼ Variations on the word do count.

Williams dons a pair of Groucho glasses and carries a stuffed duck with a word tucked in its mouth as props to explain the original *You Bet Your Life* TV show.

TIP #47: The Marker & Water Trick

Game Categories:

☐ Opener ☐ Team-building
☐ Energizer ☐ Review
☐ Communication ☑ Topical: Train-the-Trainer

■ **Purpose:** To demonstrate to future instructors how training changes individuals and entire organizations.

■ **Time Required:** Five minutes.

■ **Size of Group:** Unlimited.

■ **Materials Required:** A glass of water. A large pitcher of water. A magic marker.

■ **The Exercise in Action:** Richard Yun a trainer for Ontario Hydro, Tiverton, Ontario, stands in front of the group at the end of his train-the-trainer class, dips a marker in a glass of water and swirls it around. As the ink from the marker colors the water, Yun explains how training has changed the skills, knowledge level, and attitude of each participant just like the marker changed the water. Then Yun pours the glass of now-colored water into a nearby pitcher of water, and as the color dilutes through the pitcher (it will change the color of the water in the pitcher substantially, but it will be lighter than the water in the glass). Yun explains how each trainee will have a similar affect as their training begins to change the workplace environment.

Yun sometimes takes the exercise a step further: He pours a glass of colored water from the pitcher, saying, "Suppose another person takes the training program." Then Yun puts another marker in the glass to color the water darker and says, "That person also gains new knowledge, is energized, and changes his behavior, then returns to the workplace." At this point, Yun pours the glass of newly colored water back into the pitcher, making the entire pitcher darker than before. Then he says, "If you repeat this process, slowly but surely the entire organization will change."

TIP #48: The Beauty of a Milk Carton

Game	☐ Opener	☐ Team-building
Categories:	☐ Energizer	☐ Review
	☑ Communication	☐ Topical:

■ **Purpose:** To emphasize the importance of writing clear, easy-to-follow directions.

■ **Time Required:** 15 to 25 minutes.

■ **Size of Group:** Unlimited.

■ **Materials Required:** A number of household items.

■ **The Exercise in Action:** In courses dealing with writing skills, Gary Ford brings to class several household items with well-written and easy-to-follow directions: milk cartons, aspirin bottles, and bottled water, for example.

On a flip chart, he copies from the items all the directions for usage ("open opposite side," "refrigerate after opening," "apply freely to affected parts," and so forth). He then asks participants to discuss the clarity of each set of instructions and lists "criteria for clarity" on a flip chart.

Ford, a bilingual training coordinator with Nintendo of America in Redmond, WA, then gives participants a sample of writing or instructions that is less clearly written, due to complex sentence construction and frequent use of the passive voice. Their task is to rewrite the sample using their "criteria for clarity" as guides.

When Ford notices participants using more complicated constructions than necessary or using passive voice instead of active, he reminds them of the simple clarity of the milk carton instructions: open opposite side.

TIP #49: The World Wide Web Review

Game	☐ Opener	☐ Team-building
Categories:	☐ Energizer	☑ Review
	☐ Communication	☐ Topical:

■ **Purpose:** To encourages trainees to build on each other's knowledge during review sessions.

■ **Time Required:** 15 to 30 minutes.

■ **Size of Group:** 12 to 30.

■ **Materials Required:** Flip-chart paper and writing materials for everyone.

■ **The Exercise in Action:** Monica Beck, a trainer with BancOne in Columbus, OH, uses mind-mapping theory for a review technique she calls "World Web."

She separates participants into groups of three to 10, and asks each group to stand in front of one of several blank posters hung on the wall. Beck then assigns each group a product, service, or work procedure discussed in class, and designates a scribe to write the object in the center of the poster with a box or bubble around it.

When Beck says begin, each team has two minutes to "web" or branch off that object any related characteristics or points they can recall from the session. When the two minutes are up, teams move on to the next poster until all teams have contributed to each review sheet. The class then reviews all the posters as a whole and makes additions or adjustments where necessary.

Have each team "web" or branch off a course subject, related characteristics or points from the session. After two minutes, have teams move on to the next poster until all teams have contributed to each review sheet.

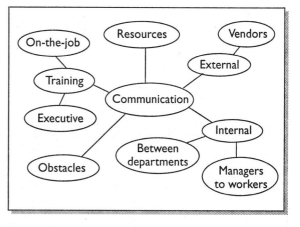

TIP #50: Interviews

**Game
Categories:**
☐ Opener   ☐ Team-building
☐ Energizer   ☑ Review
☑ Communication   ☐ Topical:

■ **Purpose:** To demonstrate the dynamics of listening and retention skills.

■ **Time Required:** 10 to 15 minutes.

■ **Size of Group:** Unlimited, but attendees should work in small groups of six.

■ **Materials Required:** None.

■ **The Exercise in Action:** Becky Russell, store manager for Microsoft in Bothell, WA, has good success with this communication exercise: One person is interviewed for five minutes on a specific topic by a team of three people, while another team of three listens to the questions and answers. At the end of the time, the "listening" team must recap what the interviewee has said in three sentences. The team asking the questions scores the other team on the accuracy of its recap. Teams are then rotated so the listeners become the interviewers, and new interviewees and topics are chosen. The team with the highest total wins.

Game Categories:	☑ **Opener** ☑ **Energizer** ☐ **Communication**	☐ **Team-building** ☐ **Review** ☐ **Topical:**

■ **Purpose:** To get trainees thinking about the training course before they even arrive.

■ **Time Required:** 10 minutes.

■ **Size of Group:** Unlimited.

■ **Materials Required:** "Admission tickets" and a set of instructions, prepared in advance by the trainer and sent to each attendee before the class begins.

■ **The Exercise in Action:** Denise Pare uses a variation of the course admission ticket concept (which many trainers use as a "tickler" to the class) to encourage students to think about what they want from a training session before they attend.

Pare, a reading curriculum coordinator at Cy-Fair Independent School District in Houston, makes tickets about the size of 3 x 5 inch note-cards and sends them — along with a brief set of instructions — to attendees a few days before her course begins. He then uses the cards as an opener in the session and refers to them over the course of the class.

The instructions:

• **First line** — Print your name.
• **Second line** — What are your expectations for the course?
• **Third line** — Explain your greatest need in the subject area.
• **Fourth line** — Get the signature of someone with whom you've shared those expectations and needs.
• **Fifth line** — Get the signature of a person who will not attend the session with whom you've promised to share something you learn from the course.

Thinking about these things prior to attending, Pare says, encourages students to consciously think about ways that a course can benefit them specifically, rather than passively waiting for knowledge to be served to them in ready-to-use portions and coming away with less than they might have because they neglected to apply lessons to their day-to-day issues.

TIP #52: Putting Things in Perspective

Game Categories:	☐ Opener	☐ Team-building
	☐ Energizer	☐ Review
	☑ Communication	☐ Topical:

■ **Purpose:** To help attendees see the importance of putting things in proper perspective when dealing with other people and sharing ideas.

■ **Time Required:** 10 to 15 minutes.

■ **Size of Group:** Unlimited.

■ **Materials Required:** A poster-sized color montage. A flashlight. A piece of cardboard with a small hole cut in it. A widely focused strobe light.

■ **The Exercise in Action:** Karen Moody, a senior analyst/meeting facilitator for Information Systems at Conoco, Houston, uses this exercise in sessions where people will be expected to share ideas and, therefore, look for new perspectives.

Moody turns out the room lights and asks participants to close their eyes. While they have their eyes closed, she hangs a large picture on a classroom wall (she uses a color montage). She then shines a flashlight through a cardboard cutout that lets only a narrow band of light hit the picture. She asks everyone to open their eyes and write down what they see.

Moody has them close their eyes again, while she shines a widely focused strobe light on the picture. She asks them to open their eyes and write down what they see.

Once again, participants are asked to close their eyes. Moody turns on the room lights this time, and has them open their eyes and write down what they see.

Moody asks trainees to share their ideas about what they saw in each case, and records that on a flip chart. She builds that input into a discussion about the importance of perspective:

▼ If we are too narrowly focused in how we look at things (flashlight), we can't see the big picture.

▼ If we have our attention placed on too many things at one time (strobe light), we become very confused.

▼ If we view things from the proper perspective (room lights), we can easily focus our attention on each area, as well as see the big picture.

Game Categories:	□ Opener □ Energizer ☑ Communication	□ Team-building □ Review □ Topical:

■ **Purpose:** To help participants get over their fear of being wrong and talk about their own ideas or experiences — in class and back on the job.

■ **Time Required:** 10 minutes.

■ **Size of Group:** Unlimited.

■ **Materials Required:** None.

■ **The Exercise in Action:** Gregory Cortopassi uses an exercise that shows answers can be different without necessarily being incorrect.

He begins by asking for a volunteer. He instructs that person to raise his or her hands, palms forward. He then puts his palms against the volunteer's and pushes, gently at first, then with increasing force. The volunteer almost always responds by pushing back (if the first one doesn't, thank the person, and move to another).

Cortopassi, a training coordinator with Teamworks Training Corp. in Boulder, CO, thanks the volunteer and asks the class a series of easy questions on which their answers generally agree: What were his instructions to the volunteer? What did the instructor do next? How did the volunteer respond?

Then Cortopassi asks his final question: Did the volunteer respond correctly to the situation? Some say yes, that there was no other logical response, that the instruction to resist was implied by the instructor's action. Others argue that instructions should be followed exactly, and none were given for the volunteer to push back.

The learning point: We're conditioned to believe there is a right and a wrong answer to everything. Sometimes, as in the demonstration, that's not true. We need to open our minds to the possibility that there may be multiple ways of responding to a situation, and many of them may be correct.

Cortopassi suggests the test of whether an idea or action is correct might be whether it achieves the desired results. That, he says, is the approach he's taking to the session. "My job is not so much to show you what's right and wrong," he tells the class, "as to assist you in exploring your responses to see if they help you get what you want. If they don't, I'll try to coach you to explore other options."

Game Categories:	☐ Opener	☐ Team-building
	☐ Energizer	☐ Review
	☐ Communication	☑ Topical: Train-the-Trainer

■ **Purpose:** To help break the ice, energize participants, and make a learning point in train-the-trainer sessions.

■ **Time Required:** About 10 minutes at the onset of a course, then a couple minutes at different times throughout a session.

■ **Materials Required:** None.

■ **The Exercise in Action:** After revisiting the idea that "anything that can go wrong, will," either Lillian Lancaster or Winzie Pollet, instructional support teachers for the training and development arm of Orange County Public Schools, Orlando, FL, shares a training experience that supports the axiom. Several volunteers are asked to recall a similar incident that occurred during the facilitation of a workshop or at some other point during their careers.

At regular intervals during their three-hour training session, a time for sharing examples of Murphy's Law is announced. "The examples often provide an opportunity for follow-up on how the situation was handled or how the problem was solved," says Lancaster. "Through this ongoing exercise, the learning point about trainer flexibility and creativity is emphasized, and a high level of interest and involvement is maintained."

Game   ☐ **Opener**   ☐ **Team-building**
Categories: ☐ **Energizer**   ☐ **Review**
               ☐ **Communication**   ☑ **Topical: Time Management**

■ **Purpose:** To facilitate discussion about the importance of time management.

■ **Time Required:** 15 to 20 minutes.

■ **Size of Group:** Unlimited.

■ **Materials Required:** A "check," made out to each participant, prepared in advance by the trainer.

■ **The Exercise in Action:** Few people have trouble deciding how to set priorities for spending money, but the same can't be said for time, even though some would argue it's a more important commodity. Joli Mauracher, a skills development specialist for GE Capital in Broomfield, CO, uses the following exercise to drive home the importance of time management:

She hands each participant a check made out to them for the amount of $86,400 (nonnegotiable, of course) and explains they have only 24 hours to spend the money. Participants then share how they plan to spend the money and each person's response is recorded on a flip chart.

When the exercise is completed, Mauracher notes that most trainees spent every penny of the check. This leads to a discussion that each day has the same amount of seconds as the check has dollars — 86,400 — and begs the question: Why we are so much more likely to prioritize how we spend our money than our time?

Game Categories:	□ Opener	□ Team-building
	□ Energizer	□ Review
	□ Communication	☑ Topical: Customer Service

■ **Purpose:** To show attendees in service training classes the benefit to the customer of using proper customer service techniques.

■ **Time Required:** 15 minutes.

■ **Size of Group:** 10 to 15

■ **Materials Required:** A questionnaire, prepared in advance by the trainer.

■ **The Exercise in Action:** Linda Lorino, training coordinator of insurance operations with Provident Mutual Life Insurance Co., Philadelphia, says a before-and-after exercise she uses in her customer service classes serves a dual purpose: It acts as a review of techniques discussed in class, and it lets people see the benefit to the customer of using proper customer service techniques.

When participants enter Lorino's classroom for a half-day session on customer service training, she gives them a questionnaire (Fig. 1) which asks them to recall a situation, good or bad, when they were a customer and how that incident changed their relationship with the business (Lorino fills out one, too).

Fig 1: Customer Relations

Think of a situation (good or bad) when you were a customer. Briefly write down:
- ▼ Where and when did the situation occur?
- ▼ What happened?
- ▼ How did you feel at the end of the situation?
- ▼ If your feelings changed, what made them change?
- ▼ Did it affect your relationship with the business? (for example, Did you decide you would definitely return to this business, or did you decide you would *never* return to this business? Or did you leave the situation feeling that it made no difference to you whether you use this particular business or a different one in the future?)
- ▼ Other comments:

During introductions, in addition to the normal reporting of name, department, years of service, etc., she asks each participant to share with the class a brief description of the incident they wrote about on the questionnaire.

At the end of the four-hour session, she has trainees take out the questionnaires again, while she passes out another form (Fig. 2). This form asks what skills discussed during the session the service provider in their examples did right or wrong. After allowing time for trainees to fill out the forms, she leads a discussion on their findings.

Fig 2: Customer Relations

Referring back to the situation you wrote about in the beginning of this session, think about the key points we discussed and answer these questions.

▼ What key points did the person you were dealing with use properly?

▼ What key point or points did the person you were dealing with not use and should have?

TIP #57: Total Recall

Game Categories:
- ☐ Opener
- ☐ Energizer
- ☐ Communication
- ☐ Team-building
- ☑ Review
- ☐ Topical:

■ **Purpose:** To lead participants through a review of "the basics" during multiple-day sessions.

■ **Time Required:** 10 minutes.

■ **Size of Group:** Unlimited, but trainees should work in small groups of three to six.

■ **Materials Required:** None.

■ **The Exercise in Action:** In multiple-day training sessions, recalling the basics from one day is often essential to the next day's learning, says Linda Duncan, a senior training officer at Norfolk Southern, McDonough, GA. So she starts each day by asking participants to write everything they can remember from the previous day, individually and without discussion.

After everyone has completed their lists, Duncan gives them time to discuss what they've recorded with others at their tables. Then the groups take turns offering information, which she records on a flip chart.

The method gets people thinking about the subject matter, she says. And because it's done without notes, it is a good test of what points the trainer is communicating well; if no participants or only a few remember a particular item, chances are it was not presented as well as it should have been.

TIP #58: Brilliant Brainstorming

Game Categories:	☐ Opener	☑ Team-building
	☑ Energizer	☐ Review
	☐ Communication	☐ Topical:

■ **Purpose:** To get team members familiar with brainstorming practices and skills.

■ **Time Required:** Five to 10 minutes.

■ **Size of Group:** Unlimited, but participants should work in small group of five or six.

■ **Materials Required:** None.

■ **The Exercise in Action:** Dottie Kinner, a senior data processing training specialist with USAA (The United Services Automobile Association) in San Antonio, TX, asks small groups to pick a four- or five-letter word. Any word will do, she says.

Once a word is chosen by each group, Kinner gives them three minutes to create sentences using each letter of their word, in sequence, as the first letter of a word in the sentence. Sentences must have proper structure, but they don't have to make sense — which adds a few laughs to the exercise. For example, a team might create a sentence from the word *MOLD* — Moonstruck Oranges Like Drinking.

The team creating the most sentences from its one word is awarded a small prize. Kinner encourages teams to pick words relating to the course content. "The exercise gives new teams a chance to develop some synergy and work on brainstorming together," a skill they'll certainly need in the future, she says.

Game   ☐ Opener   ☑ Team-building
Categories: ☐ Energizer   ☐ Review
                  ☐ Communication   ☐ Topical

■ **Purpose:** To convince attendees they can solve problems with teamwork more quickly and easily than they can by trudging along solo.

■ **Time Required:** 10 to 20 minutes.

■ **Size of Group:** 12 or more participants working in small groups of four.

■ **Materials Required:** An object brought by each trainee. A shoe box.

■ **The Exercise in Action:** Angie Rohlman, a project manager at Kimball International, Jasper, IN, sends class registrants a note a few days in advance of courses asking them to bring a small object to be placed in a shoe box with items brought in by others.

At the start of the session, participants get 60 seconds to look in the box and then have a minute to list on paper as many items as they can remember.

Rohlman then divides the students into groups of four and gives them another minute to generate a list of the contents of the box as a group. They invariably do better, she says, which makes for an effective opener in team-building courses.

Game Categories:

☑ Opener ☐ Team-building
☑ Energizer ☐ Review
☐ Communication ☐ Topical:

■ **Purpose:** To demonstrate that listening is more than a passive skill, and that eyes can be as important as ears in perceiving a message.

■ **Time Required:** Five minutes.

■ **Size of Group:** Unlimited.

■ **Materials Required:** Copies of the American Sign Language (ASL) alphabet for all participants. A presenter who is familiar with ASL.

■ **The Exercise in Action:** At the outset of any class, there's always some last-minute shuffling around as trainees settle into their chairs, pull out pens and notebooks, and so forth. This activity often continues even after the trainer begins the session, with trainees assuming they'll get any valuable information by casually listening.

To demonstrate otherwise, Nina Hollingsworth, a trainer with Mead Coated Board, Phenix City, AL, asks an employee who "speaks" sign language to introduce the course. Each attendee is given a copy of the American Sign Language alphabet and asked to record what they pick up. The employee slowly signs the word "welcome." That, Hollingsworth says, is when all extraneous shuffling stops, as the trainees realize they cannot rely on their ears alone to "listen" to the introduction.

After the exercise, Hollingsworth, leads the class through a discussion on the value of using all available resources in order to give someone your full attention.

TIP #61: Story Time

Game Categories:

☐ Opener   ☐ Team-building
☐ Energizer   ☐ Review
☐ Communication   ☑ Topical: Orientation

■ **Purpose:** To help new employees develop friendships and learn about each other during orientation training.

■ **Time Required:** About 15 to 20 minutes at the beginning and end of each orientation session.

■ **Size of Group:** Five to 10.

■ **Materials Required:** None.

■ **The Exercise in Action:** Heidi Mattson, an education specialist at the University of Wisconsin Credit Union in Madison, WI, uses a variation of the "share something about yourself" technique she calls "Story Time."

At the beginning and end of each eight-hour training day, Mattson presents a new topic to the class and asks each participant to share a related short personal story with the class. Possible topics are best weather story (tornado, hurricane, blizzard), most embarrassing moment, worst haircut, pet/animal story, worst/best date, ugliest childhood outfit that your mother made you wear, or a story about running into someone in an unexpected place.

To keep the exercise fresh after a few days, she asks trainees to tell either a true story or a lie and encourages the others to guess which it is.

TIP #62: Stupid Questions

Game Categories:
- ☑ Opener
- ☐ Energizer
- ☐ Communication
- ☐ Team-building
- ☐ Review
- ☐ Topical:

■ **Purpose:** To help trainees overcome the fear of speaking up and perhaps looking foolish in class.

■ **Time Required:** 15 minutes.

■ **Size of Group:** Eight to 10.

■ **Materials Required:** None.

■ **The Exercise in Action:** Every trainer has repeated the classroom cliche, "There's no such thing as a stupid question." But the simple fact is some participants *are* reluctant to ask questions for fear of sounding foolish, and that can lead to a serious lack of interaction in a session.

To get attendees over that hump at the outset of a course, Darren Patton reads aloud a list of some of the silliest, most irrelevant questions he's ever had to answer in a corporate classroom. Examples include, "What color were the walls in this room before they painted them blue?" and, "How many vacation days do you get per year?"

Once the list is read, Patton, a trainer with The Vanguard Group, Wayne, PA, asks small groups to have some fun and come up with a single, bizarre question to share with the large group. The query judged most irrelevant by the entire class wins that group a small prize.

"After a few laughs, people start realizing that nothing they ask can be as silly or irrelevant as the previous questions," Patton says. "That tends to make the class more comfortable with voicing questions later in the session."

TIP #63: Three-Way Role-Play

Game Categories:	☐ Opener	☑ Team-building
	☐ Energizer	☐ Review
	☐ Communication	☑ Topical: Sales

■ **Purpose:** To make role-plays easier and less threatening for sales people.

■ **Time Required:** 20 minutes.

■ **Size of Group:** Unlimited, but trainees should work in small groups of three.

■ **Materials Required:** None.

■ **The Exercise in Action:** The two-person role-play has always been a cornerstone of effective sales training. But Mike Kaska, director of training for international operations at John Hancock Financial Services in Boston, believes the three-person approach — with one trainee acting as a coach — makes it easier for trainees to absorb the learning points they might have missed while in the heat of the moment of a role-play.

In this scenario, one trainee plays the role of salesperson, another the role of the prospect, and the third person plays the role of an observer or "coach" who can supply advice to the salesperson whenever needed. The roles are rotated until everyone on a team has a chance to play each role at least once. With this arrangement, learning takes place in three ways, says Kaska:

▼ Learning by doing (salesperson).

▼ Learning by listening (prospect).

▼ Learning by observation, analysis, and feedback (coach).

TIP #64: What's in a Name?

Game Categories:	☑ **Opener**	☑ **Team-building**
	☐ **Energizer**	☐ **Review**
	☐ **Communication**	☐ **Topical:**

■ **Purpose:** To help participants relate with more ease at the start of class. (This exercise is tailor-made for team-building sessions.)

■ **Time Required:** 10 to 15 minutes.

■ **Size of Group:** Unlimited.

■ **Materials Required:** Flip-chart paper.

■ **The Exercise in Action:** Yvonne Thornton, a training specialist with UT Southwestern in Dallas, asks participants, one at a time, to write their first names on a flip chart at the front of class. They're also asked to write a nickname they've had in their lives, explaining the nickname's origin as they write. Someone nicknamed "Bones," for instance, might trace it back to being skinny as a child.

Thornton says the exercise is well-suited for team-building efforts within departments because "it helps team members begin training with reduced tension and increased rapport. It also provides more insight into personalities and backgrounds." Many times participants are called by their old nicknames throughout the rest of the session, she says.

TIP #65: Coins and Catch Phrases

Game Categories:	☐ Opener	☐ Team-building
	☑ Energizer	☐ Review
	☐ Communication	☐ Topical:

■ **Purpose:** To initiate class breaks and help make learning points throughout a course.

■ **Time Required:** Five minutes.

■ **Size of Group:** Unlimited.

■ **Materials Required:** A handful of coins.

■ **The Exercise in Action:** Before her training sessions start, Jane Muegge, a rural community advisor for the Ontario Ministry of Agriculture in Clinton, Ontario, randomly tapes various coins to the bottom of participants' chairs. At a point where the group needs an energizer or a stretch, Muegge asks trainees to look under their chairs. She asks what they find, then asks how those various pennies, nickels, and dimes can be characterized by one word. When she gets the word she wants — change — she springs it on them: "And in order to make change(s) in the company, we need to get up off of our seats." Attendees then head off to break.

TIP #66: Alphabet Soup

Game Categories:

☑ **Opener** ☐ **Team-building**
☑ **Energizer** ☐ **Review**
☐ **Communication** ☐ **Topical:**

■ **Purpose:** To help large groups mix and mingle.

■ **Time Required:** 10 to 15 minutes.

■ **Size of Group:** No more than 26 (but certain letters of the alphabet can be repeated if the group is larger).

■ **Materials Required:** One Post-it Note with a letter of the alphabet on it for every participant, prepared in advance by the trainer.

■ **The Exercise in Action:** Rhonda Gordon, human resources training manager for Bureau of National Affairs, Washington, DC, conceived of the following opener when preparing a training course for 26 people. The number 26 sparked an idea and the "Alphabet Opener" was born, but she says it can be used for smaller or larger classes if the instructor prepares properly. Here are the instructions for the exercise:

Give all participants a Post-it Note with a large letter printed on it, and ask them to place the letter on their shirt fronts. Avoid letters like Q, X, or Z, and offer about twice as many consonants as vowels. Gordon recommends making the vowels a different color from the consonants so they're easily recognizable.

Tell participants they have five minutes to form any word with at least three other people, but explain that longer words are fine. Gordon says participants are rarely left out — and when they are, other groups often break their words and make a new one to include the additional person — but she keeps extra Post-its with letters handy and if a straggler is spotted, she steps in to ask another group to break their word and make a new one. Extra vowels and the letter "S" for making plurals work best, she says.

After five minutes, give each group a sheet of flip-chart paper to post and ask them to form a sentence or a phrase using the word to describe their expectations of the course.

TIP #67: Attitude Is Everything

Game Categories: ☐ Opener   ☑ Team-building
☐ Energizer   ☐ Review
☐ Communication   ☐ Topical:

■ **Purpose:** To help trainees realize that the *attitude* of team members has more to do with the team being successful than any knowledge or individual skill any member may bring.

■ **Time Required:** 10 to 15 minutes.

■ **Size of Group:** Unlimited.

■ **Materials Required:** Flip chart and paper.

■ **The Exercise in Action:** Debbie London Baker, president of London Baker Group, Tampa, FL, asks a group to brainstorm for five minutes on the qualities of the ideal team member and lists the qualities on a flip chart. The qualities range from having an excellent sense of humor, to being very serious about their work, to being an excellent goal setter and time manager. She then presents definitions for "skill" and "attitude" and has the group come to agreement: A skill is something we learn, like riding a bike or speaking another language. And attitude is how we feel emotionally about those skills.

The group then decides if the items on the list are skills or attitudes (some may be both). Generally, attitudes dominate (approximately 85 percent to 15 percent). London Baker then leads a discussion on the implications of the lists.

TIP #68: Going Behind their Backs

Game Categories:

- [ ] Opener
- [x] Energizer
- [ ] Communication
- [x] Team-building
- [ ] Review
- [ ] Topical:

■ **Purpose:** To help participants feel great about themselves and each other, and perhaps improve interdepartmental relationships.

■ **Time Required:** 10 to 20 minutes.

■ **Size of Group:** Unlimited.

■ **Materials Required:** Small slips of paper and writing utensils for everyone.

■ **The Exercise in Action:** Gary Ellis, in information systems training and support with Lennox Industries, Urbandale, IA, has attendees tape sheets of paper to each others' backs, then gives them time to mingle and write compliments about each other on those sheets.

Ellis compares the exercise to the tradition of signing high school yearbooks. He sometimes uses this energizer as a transition from one section of a training session to another or as a way to build camaraderie in a group. In those situations the exercise takes about 10 minutes. When the training content is related to improving communication or increasing cooperation within teams, he sometimes devotes up to 20 minutes for this activity.

TIP #69: Baseball Review

Game Categories:	☐ Opener	☐ Team-building
	☐ Energizer	☑ Review
	☐ Communication	☐ Topical:

■ **Purpose:** To use the familiar game of baseball as a backdrop to a competitive review session.

■ **Time Required:** 20 to 30 minutes (or longer, depending on the amount of material to be reviewed).

■ **Size of Group:** 12 or more.

■ **Materials Required:** Masking tape. Colored poster board. One large fuzzy die.

■ **The Exercise in Action:** America's pastime becomes the basis of a review game in Catherine Bolin's sessions. She clears the center of the room (or just a baseline path if conditions don't permit clearing the entire floor) to make a baseball diamond. Then, she uses masking tape to connect "bases" of colored poster board; bases alone work fine if tape removal poses a problem.

Two teams are chosen, and each is seated in a "dugout" of chairs on opposing baselines in "batting order." The teams create names and logos. Depending on time constraints, participants may design team pennants and flip-chart-sized banners.

Bolin, a chemistry instructor at Duke Power/Catawba Nuclear Station, York, SC, tosses a coin to choose which team is first at the plate. She then "pitches" a question. Teammates are allowed to shout hints to the batter. If the batter answers correctly, a large die — the kind that typically is hung from car mirrors — is tossed. If a one comes up, the player advances to first base, two equals a double, three a triple, and four a home run. Five indicates a foul, and the player must field another question. There are two ways to be put out: by rolling a six on the die or by answering a question incorrectly. Players who reach a base advance when "forced" by the next runner.

After three outs, the other team takes a turn at bat. The process is repeated for as many innings as time permits. Score is kept, to keep things lively, but both teams are awarded prizes with the explanation that everyone who learns is a winner.

Game   ☑ **Opener**   ☐ **Team-building**
Categories: ☐ **Energizer**   ☐ **Review**
                 ☐ **Communication** ☑ **Topical: Diversity**

■ **Purpose:** To show participants how appropriate or inappropriate it is to make assumptions about others.

■ **Time Required:** 10 minutes at the outset of class.

■ **Size of Group:** 10 to 30.

■ **Materials Required:** Slips of paper, each with the name of a different participant written on it, prepared in advance by the trainer.

■ **The Exercise in Action:** Leslie Huerter, religious education director for St. Mary's Church, gives everyone a slip of paper with the name of another person, which they're not to reveal to the other participants. Attendees are asked to observe their "designated person" throughout the day and write down positive observations and assumptions as they go along. At some point, she has each person note outloud the qualities they've observed on index cards that are later given to the other person. "This activity is great for helping people see themselves as others see them," says Huerter.

TIP #71: Silent Birthdays

Game	☐ Opener	☑ Team-building
Categories:	☐ Energizer	☐ Review
	☑ Communication	☐ Topical:

■ **Purpose:** To shake participants out of old communication and leadership styles.

■ **Time Required:** Five to 10 minutes.

■ **Size of Group:** Unlimited.

■ **Materials Required:** None.

■ **The Exercise in Action:** Near the outset of her communication courses, Karen Shuler, executive director of Humanscope Inc., McClellanville, SC, asks the entire group (or small groups of 10, if the class is especially large) to line up in ascending order by their birth dates. The catch? They cannot speak to each other.

Shuler allows five to 10 minutes for the exercise, monitoring the frustration level as time runs out and jumping in with a tip or two if need be. Typically, a leader will emerge and realize that the group can communicate via their hands or other tools lying about the room such as pen and paper.

When time is up, she has the group (or each small group) call out its lineup.

The exercise is a quick means of highlighting topics to be covered in class, such as the need to find new ways of communicating when working in a team environment, how leadership issues emerge, which styles of leadership work or don't work, and the importance of making sure everyone is communicating the same way.

Game	☐ **Opener**	☑ **Team-building**
Categories:	☐ **Energizer**	☐ **Review**
	☐ **Communication**	☐ **Topical:**

■ **Purpose:** To help groups in team-training sessions learn from past experiences.

■ **Time Required:** 15 minutes.

■ **Size of Group:** Unlimited.

■ **Materials Required:** Post-it Notes.

■ **The Exercise in Action:** Gail Melin, a team trainer with 3M Tape Manufacturing in Hutchinson, MN, first asks participants to think of any team they've been a part of in the past, and using one color of Post-it Notes, list all of the positive or effective characteristics of that team (one thought/idea per note). Using another color Post-it, they're asked to list the ineffective behaviors.

She then hangs a wall-size model of a team's typical development cycle, with phases including team formation and growth, stagnation, and breakthroughs. Participants are asked to stick their Post-its on the phase in the model where they observed that behavior on their former teams. "The result is a better illustration of where and how many teams get stuck, or development gets stunted," and how improvement happens, Melin says.

Discussion and debriefing that follows usually centers on how team members can become part of solutions. She also has participants develop lists of proactive and reactive guidelines to use on their current teams.

TIP #73: Dealing with Differences

**Game
Categories:**

☐ Opener   ☐ Team-building
☐ Energizer   ☐ Review
☐ Communication   ☑ Topical: Diversity

■ **Purpose:** To get people thinking about differences and similarities between themselves and other course participants.

■ **Time Required:** 10 minutes.

■ **Size of Group:** Unlimited, but participants should work in small groups of four.

■ **Materials Required:** None.

■ **The Exercise in Action:** Susan Johnson, a manager of youth programs at the National Wildlife Federation, Arlington, VA, divides participants into groups of four and gives them two minutes to discover two ways that all of them are alike and four ways they're different. The time limit is optional, Johnson says, but tends to add a level of excitement to the exercise. "Easy" answers, such as noting that all members are wearing shoes, are discouraged.

From there, it's easy to spring into a discussion of how the groups benefit from their differences and similarities, how those characteristics apply to actual workplace situations, or simply to recognize the importance of acknowledging that diversity exists.

TIP #74: Team Drawings

Game Categories:	☐ Opener	☑ Team-building
	☑ Energizer	☐ Review
	☐ Communication	☐ Topical:

■ **Purpose:** To set a tone of openness and fun for a team-building session.

■ **Time Required:** 30 minutes.

■ **Size of Group:** Unlimited.

■ **Materials Required:** Lots of colored markers. Flip-chart paper.

■ **The Exercise in Action:** At the outset of team-building courses, Marty Jordan, a senior consultant with Amoco Oil, Chicago, IL, provides lots of colored markers and gives each participant a sheet of flip-chart paper. He asks participants to divide the sheet into quarters and label the quadrants:
   ▼ **Upper left:** Strengths I bring to the team
   ▼ **Upper right:** Ways I might hinder the team
   ▼ **Lower left:** What I need from others to do my best
   ▼ **Lower right:** Hobbies, interests, outside activities
Participants are asked to use drawings (no words are allowed) in each quadrant. He gives them 20 to 30 minutes to complete their drawings.

Jordan completes a flip-chart sheet, too, and "models" the introduction. He then has each person come up and share his or her chart and tape it up on a classroom wall.

Using drawings instead of words, taps trainees' creative juices and allows people to share much about themselves in a way that doesn't make them feel as self-conscious as they might if they verbally described the same attributes, Jordan says. He leaves the drawings up throughout the session as conversation-starters during breaks and lunch.

TIP #75: New Employee Egg Hunt

Game Categories:	☐ Opener ☑ Energizer ☐ Communication	☐ Team-building ☐ Review ☑ Topical: Orientation

■ **Purpose:** To put a colorful spin on orientation training.

■ **Time Required:** 20 minutes.

■ **Size of Group:** Unlimited.

■ **Materials Required:** A multitude of colored, plastic Easter eggs. Slips of paper with questions on them to slip inside the eggs, prepared in advance by the trainer.

■ **The Exercise in Action:** Before orientation sessions, Donna Loughridge, a systems trainer with MCI Telecommunications in Colorado Springs, CO, writes questions on small pieces of paper, then slips them inside eggs. Loughridge then hides the eggs in a common area, such as the cafeteria, and asks participants to hunt for them.

When an employee finds an egg, the mission is to answer the question inside. This often requires the finder to locate a particular person or department within the company. For example, if the question is, "How many employees work in the packaging area?" the seeker will have to speak to someone working in that area, possibly the supervisor. This, Loughridge says, creates a familiarity with where various people and functions are located in the company, while helping the new associate learn some names and faces from various areas.

After finding an answer, the employee returns to the egg-hunt area to find another egg. After all the eggs have been found and the corresponding questions answered, Loughridge asks participants to share their newfound knowledge with the group. The participant with the most questions correctly answered wins a small prize.

Game Categories:	☐ Opener	☐ Team-building
	☑ Energizer	☐ Review
	☐ Communication	☐ Topical:

■ **Purpose:** To challenge participants' ability to think creatively.

■ **Time Required:** 15 minutes.

■ **Size of Group:** Unlimited.

■ **Materials Required:** Scrap paper for everyone.

■ **The Exercise in Action:** The next time you want to put a different spin on a tired exercise and challenge participants creatively, consider the approach of trainer Tony Manning.

Give each participant a single sheet of paper and ask them to make a plane that flies. Each person will more than likely be successful and also be able to demonstrate for others having problems. Next ask that they use a fresh sheet of paper to create a new flying machine. Allow them the same amount of time to look for an entirely new design — a revolutionary new airborne machine that must fly.

In all likelihood, very few will succeed. Most will build upon or slightly alter the conventional design. When all have finished, take a piece of paper, crush it into a ball and throw it across the room. Explain that the problem was to create a new flying machine, not to repeat more of the same. A ball of paper will fly. It doesn't matter whether something fits our concept, what is critical is whether or not that something fits the parameters of the individual problem — or the valid requirements of the participant's customer or client.

TIP #77: Brick Wall

Game Categories:	☐ Opener	☐ Team-building
	☐ Energizer	☐ Review
	☐ Communication	☑ Topical: Customer Service

■ **Purpose:** To illustrate the barriers employees often encounter in trying to serve customers efficiently.

■ **Time Required:** 20 to 30 minutes.

■ **Size of Group:** Eight to 15.

■ **Materials Required:** A supply of cardboard bricks.

■ **The Exercise in Action:** Pam Griffin creates a "brick wall" to show trainees how to overcome the barriers to customer service.

Griffin, a senior operations analyst with the Georgia Department of Labor in Atlanta, builds the wall out of cardboard bricks purchased at a local toy store. As the training begins, she explains that some of the bricks represent "immovable" laws or regulations that govern her industry. Some are there because of state and local policies and some because of employees' own inflexibility concerning policies or about "going beyond the call" of regular duties.

As participants offer their solutions to flaws in the system, they are invited to come up and knock holes in the cardboard wall to illustrate a breakthrough, whether as the result of a new policy or as a new way of thinking about a situation.

Sometimes, Griffin says, playful trainees come up during breaks and rearrange remaining bricks into new designs — and she uses that as a teaching point, too. "I use this spontaneous action to demonstrate how we often replace one barrier with another without realizing it."

She says the brick wall idea can also be used in other training programs to illustrate barriers built by trainers, trainees, or outside influences such as supervisors or managers who fail to support training back on the job.

Game   ☐ Opener   ☑ Team-building
Categories: ☑ Energizer   ☐ Review
                      ☐ Communication   ☐ Topical:

■ **Purpose:** To energize and build teamwork within a group.

■ **Time Required:** Five minutes.

■ **Size of Group:** Five to 20.

■ **Materials Required:** Flash cubes (the type that flash four times; the taller bar type will not work) and a pencil eraser.

■ **The Exercise in Action:** On the bottom of each flash cube are four curved slots. Across the middle of each slot, inside the flash cube, is a very thin piece of wire. That wire is the trigger which ignites the flash. Anything that presses against the wire will cause one of the four flashes to ignite.

Use a scissors to cut a wedge off the end of a pencil eraser. This makes an excellent "button" for setting off a flash. Insert the wedge into one of the slots, but don't press it until you have positioned the exercise, which creates an effective (if illusionary) illustration of the power of teamwork:

Ask participants to stand in a circle and hold hands. Stand in the center, making it clear you must be careful not to touch anyone, and instruct them to shuffle their feet rapidly. Hold the flash cube between your finger and thumb. After about a minute, reach out and make contact with someone in the circle. At the same time, press the "button." The lesson of this trick, of course, is that working together we can accomplish things that seem (and, in fact are) impossible to achieve alone.

The cube trick also works as a "magic volunteer finder." Simply move among attendees, holding out the cube like a divining tool of some sort. Ignite the flash, choosing — seemingly randomly — the next volunteer. A single cube can be used four times for either trick.

**Game
Categories:**

☐ Opener ☐ Team-building
☐ Energizer ☑ Review
☐ Communication ☐ Topical:

■ **Purpose:** To motivate trainees to complete a successful review session.

■ **Time Required:** 10 minutes.

■ **Size of Group:** Unlimited.

■ **Materials Required:** Slips of paper, each with one ingredient to making chocolate cookies written on it, prepared in advance by the trainer. A large mixing bowl. Real chocolate chip cookies.

■ **The Exercise in Action:** Chocolate chip cookies are, arguably, the ultimate classroom motivator (as is any type of food, for that matter). Here's how Lauren Irwin, training manager for FAA Credit Union, uses that idea during class:

Irwin places several slips of paper in a bowl, each listing an ingredient to a recipe for chocolate chip cookies. When participants answer questions correctly, they take an ingredient slip out of the bowl and pin it to a posted picture of a chocolate chip cookie. When a group answers enough questions to empty the bowl and complete the recipe, Irwin brings out a large tray of cookies as a reward.

**Chocolate Chip
Cookie Motivator**

Have participants pin cookie recipe ingredients on a cookie drawn on a flip-chart when they answer questions correctly. When all of the questions are answered, reward the class with a plateful of cookies.

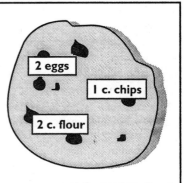

TIP #80: 'I Do Not Like Them, Sam I Am...'

Game Categories:

☐ Opener ☐ Team-building
☐ Energizer ☐ Review
☑ Communication ☑ Topical: Customer Service

■ **Purpose:** To help attendees of customer service or general communication training courses hone their voice clarity, tone, and pacing skills.

■ **Time Required:** 15 to 25 minutes.

■ **Size of Group:** 10 to 15.

■ **Materials Required:** A selection of books by Dr. Suess. A tape recorder.

■ **The Exercise in Action:** Dr. Suess's children's book, *Green Eggs and Ham*, proves an effective and entertaining training tool in Rita Dillow's training for customer service representatives.

Dillow, a training manager at *The Florida Times-Union*, Jacksonville, FL, uses the reading exercise to help representatives improve voice tone, pacing, and clarity, which she finds occasionally need refreshing. She also uses the books in more general courses about communication skills.

Each of the participants' readings is taped, and then constructively critiqued by the rest of the group. "Participants really have a good time with the exercise," Dillow says, "and each tries to outdo the other in technique."

TIP #81: A Letter from the President

**Game
Categories:**
☑ **Opener**
☐ **Energizer**
☐ **Communication**
☐ **Team-building**
☐ **Review**
☐ **Topical:**

■ **Purpose:** To inspire trainees about the training course — even before it begins.

■ **Time Required:** Five minutes.

■ **Size of Group:** Unlimited.

■ **Materials Required:** A letter from the president of the company, prepared in advance.

■ **The Exercise in Action:** Katherine Bird, training specialist for Fidelity Federal Bank, sends a letter from the company president to all participants prior to a course to inspire people a little before they ever enter the classroom.

The letter consists of two paragraphs: one explains why the president feels the course is important to business success; the other explains why they've been invited to the program. Bird then uses the letter as an opener to the session.

TIP #82: Funny Pages

Game Categories:

☐ Opener   ☐ Team-building
☑ Energizer   ☐ Review
☐ Communication ☐ Topical:

■ **Purpose:** To encourage interaction between attendees and build different small groups for exercises.

■ **Time Required:** 15 minutes.

■ **Size of Group:** Can vary, according to trainer's need.

■ **Materials Required:** Selected comic strips, cut into individual panels in advance by the trainer.

■ **The Exercise in Action:** Using comic strips can make dividing large groups into several smaller ones fast and enjoyable, says MaryAnn Dana an associate project manager with Craft and Miertschin in Houston. She separates the panels of several comics, shuffles them, and hands one to each student. Their job is to find the other panels to complete their strips.

There are several ways to apply the technique, depending on whether your primary objective is to form groups, or whether you're using the exercise as a mixer, too.

For maximum interaction of participants, use different issues of the same comic strip. For example, to divide a class of 20 into five groups of four, distribute squares from five *Calvin and Hobbes* cartoons, each having four separate panels. The difficulty of the exercise forces greater interaction. If creating groups is your primary interest, make it easy. One set of people gets *Peanuts* pictures, another gets *Sally Forth*, and so on.

The method is flexible enough to fit many small group sizes. For larger subsets, look to the Sunday paper, which often features comics with 10 or more panels. Three or four panels is typical of a weekday feature.

TIP #83: What Will the Future Hold?

Game Categories:

☑ **Opener**   ☑ **Team-building**
☐ **Energizer**   ☐ **Review**
☐ **Communication** ☐ **Topical:**

■ **Purpose:** To help participants judge themselves in a positive light.

■ **Time Required:** 15 to 20 minutes.

■ **Size of Group:** Unlimited.

■ **Materials Required:** None.

■ **The Exercise in Action:** Use this futuristic scenario as an ice breaker or point of departure in your courses, suggests W. Greg Lanier, a training specialist with Duke Power Co. He reads them this text:

"In the somewhat distant future, people begin to explore the galaxy and to colonize other planets. In view of the great distances and traveling times involved, potential colonists may be put in suspended animation for transport. Some colonies certainly receive more colonists than can be accommodated, so there will be warehouses full of frozen people, ready to be defrosted as needed...if ever.

"You are a colonist about to be put in cryogenic suspension. You are filling out a lengthy form in which all of your demographic and professional characteristics are listed. You come to a question that asks you to list up to six adjective-noun combinations (such as "hard worker" or "good parent") which describe you as a person. What would you list? What qualities do you have that would make someone else decide that you are worth thawing out?"

He has participants write out their list of six characteristics and then discuss them with each other. In larger classes, it is best done in small breakout groups; in small classes, a round-robin works well.

TIP #84: Road Map

Game Categories:	☐ Opener	☐ Team-building
	☐ Energizer	☐ Review
	☐ Communication	☑ Topical: Train-the-Trainer

■ **Purpose:** To show prospective trainers the importance of giving clear instructions.

■ **Time Required:** 10 to 15 minutes.

■ **Size of Group:** Unlimited.

■ **Materials Required:** None.

■ **The Exercise in Action:** If you're training trainers (line managers, subject-matter experts, or other part-timers) to deliver your courses, teaching them how to give clear instructions is one of the most important first steps. Here's an exercise that demonstrates the importance of a delivery step many people take for granted:

Ask participants to imagine that, following the training program, they have invited the group to their homes for a small gathering. Allow three to five minutes for everyone to write directions to their homes.

Then summarize the various methods participants use to give directions. People generally give directions (and instructions) the way they like to receive them. Directions may be communicated by drawing a map; by using a sequential description ("As you exit the parking lot turn right, go two blocks to the stop sign and turn left on Powers Rd."); or by associating the route with landmarks.

Ask participants which method they considered most helpful. Then tell them that it depends on the individual. Some of us favor precise instructions, others prefer references to landmarks because they can be seen more readily than street signs, and others function better with a map. And some find an overview at the outset helpful, such as, "I live about five miles north of the office and it should take you about 15 minutes to get there."

The activity brings home the fact that we need to be very conscious not only about how we give information or instructions, but how individual trainees best assimilate information.

TIP #85: Sound and Motion

Game	☑ Opener	☐ Team-building
Categories:	☑ Energizer	☐ Review
	☐ Communication	☐ Topical:

■ **Purpose:** To help participants introduce themselves to one another...and to *remember* those names.

■ **Time Required:** 15 minutes.

■ **Size of Group:** Eight to 20.

■ **Materials Required:** None.

■ **The Exercise in Action:** With groups of 20 or less, Bryan Cooper uses an introduction that energizes while aiding participants' recall of their class members' names.

Cooper, a claims trainer at Nationwide Inc., Columbus, OH, asks attendees to stand in a circle and introduce themselves by first name and one adjective that begins with the same letter as their name — for example, "I'm brilliant Bryan." He asks each person to add a simple movement or gesture, such as a bow, a two-handed wave, or a dance step.

Participants are asked to repeat the names, adjectives, and actions of all preceding group members before adding their own. This makes people uncomfortable at first, but they tend to loosen up as introductions progress. In the end, participants are laughing and having fun. And, on a more practical note, they've received two aids (an alliterative word and a silly action) to help them link names with faces.

Game Categories:	☐ Opener	☑ Team-building
	☐ Energizer	☐ Review
	☐ Communication	☑ Topical: Change Management

■ **Purpose:** To show a group the consequences of acting (or not acting) together and to make a point about responding to change.

■ **Time Required:** 10 to 15 minutes.

■ **Size of Group:** 10 to 25.

■ **Materials Required:** None.

■ **The Exercise in Action:** Mary Todd, training director at the Shadow Mountain Institute, uses a technique she calls a "group juggle" to make a variety of learning points.

Todd has a group of 10 to 25 people stand in a circle and asks each person to take a turn juggling an item as best they can — throw it up and down, throw it from one hand to another — then toss it to another group member until everyone has handled the item.

Todd then asks the group to remember the juggling pattern used — the number of times someone threw the item up, and who they threw it to — and to repeat the pattern several times to develop competency. Then without announcing it, she adds a second item and then a third — like a rubber chicken — and has the group repeating three patterns simultaneously.

Todd says the activity makes several learning points:

1. Competency must be developed gradually.

2. People respond differently to change.

3. Some trainees focus on individuals who drop the item or err somehow in the process; others focus on the efficiency of the group system.

4. Individual styles impact the acceptance of change, as does the amount of interest paid to the goal versus the process.

TIP #87: Tied Up in Knots

Game Categories:	☐ Opener	☑ Team-building
	☐ Energizer	☐ Review
	☑ Communication	☑ Topical: Problem-solving

■ **Purpose:** To reinforce problem-solving, communication, and team-work skills.

■ **Time Required:** 15 minutes.

■ **Size of Group:** 10 to 25.

■ **Materials Required:** None.

■ **The Exercise in Action:** Dave Carl, manager of training and development for QuickTrip Corp., asks teams of five to 10 participants to form a "human knot."

To begin, he asks the group to form a circle and clasp hands with two other people *across* the circle. At that point the group is a tangle of hands and arms, and Carl asks them to unravel themselves and return the circle to its original shape *without* releasing hands.

He says the process demonstrates the importance of communication and teamwork to accomplish what *appears* to be a relatively simple goal.

TIP #88: A Chance to Win Millions

Game   ☐ **Opener**   ☐ **Team-building**
Categories: ☑ **Energizer**   ☐ **Review**
            ☐ **Communication** ☐ **Topical:**

■ **Purpose:** To encourage rapt attention by ratcheting up the typical reward for doing so.

■ **Time Required:** 10 minutes.

■ **Size of Group:** 15 to 20.

■ **Materials Required:** A lottery ticket for every attendee, purchased in advance by the trainer.

■ **The Exercise in Action:** Miniature candy bars hold a time-honored place as a motivating reward for trainees. So imagine the payoff if you raise the stakes...

Todd Richardson, national sales and product trainer at Philips Consumer Electronics, Knoxville, TN, buys enough lottery tickets to provide one for each attendee. At the beginning of a session, he announces there will be a quiz later, and anyone who scores 100 percent will have the opportunity to win millions. On occasion he gives the "quiz" to participants right after the announcement, and invites them to record answers as they hear them during class discussion — a great way to fight "doze-off syndrome." Successful participants receive a lottery ticket, along with congratulations and a good-luck wish.

The method can be varied a number of ways, including using scratch-off instant lotteries. The prizes are smaller, but the odds of winning much greater — in a class of 15 or more, chances are quite high that one or more people will instantly win a small amount.

TIP #89: Get the Monkey Off Your Back

Game Categories:	☐ Opener	☐ Team-building
	☐ Energizer	☑ Review
	☐ Communication	☐ Topical:

■ **Purpose:** To lighten review sessions.

■ **Time Required:** 10 to 15 minutes.

■ **Size of Group:** Unlimited.

■ **Materials Required:** A toy monkey.

■ **The Exercise in Action:** Students are often reluctant to ask what they feel are ignorant questions for fear of appearing foolish in front of peers, says Carol Schumacher, a training officer at the Arizona Department of Economic Security, Phoenix. The truth is, she tells attendees, if you are confused on a point, others probably share your confusion. So she saves time at the end of a session for a little "monkey business."

When the session is drawing to a close, Schumacher introduces her stuffed toy monkey — the kind with the long arms and Velcro hands. For fun, she can introduce it as Mr. Problem, Mr. Nasty Issue, or by any other name that indicates its symbolic role as the "monkey on your back."

She tells attendees she will pass the monkey around. Participants with unanswered questions or who are confused about some aspect of a lesson are encouraged to wrap the monkey's arms around their necks, describe the situation or problem to the rest of the class, and ask the class for assistance.

Once a participant's questions are answered, he takes the monkey off his back and passes it along. The exercise ends when everyone has been offered a turn.

The method is high-energy, Schumacher says, and the ridiculousness of the approach helps people get past their inhibitions to ask questions.

Game   ☐ **Opener**   ☐ **Team-building**
Categories: ☐ **Energizer**   ☐ **Review**
                  ☑ **Communication**   ☐ **Topical:**

■ **Purpose:** To encourage and teach positive communication between participants.

■ **Time Required:** 10 minutes.

■ **Size of Group:** Unlimited.

■ **Materials Required:** A flip-chart page. Post-it Notes.

■ **The Exercise in Action:** Many people are reluctant to compliment others freely, says Kim Weiss, a computer training specialist at Nation's Bank, Charlotte, NC. But peer encouragement is a powerful learning stimulant. To facilitate that kind of exchange and to teach attendees to positively communicate with one another, Weiss creates a "post office" in her classroom.

The post office consists of a flip-chart page (or pages) marked with a square for each participant. The instructor puts an attendee's name under each square.

Post-it Notes are available to all participants, either as part of their training packets or at each classroom table. Weiss encourages participants to write down positive comments about fellow students as they interact with them, and post them openly for all to read during course breaks.

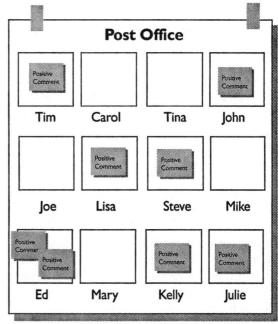

**Game
Categories:**

☐ Opener ☑ Team-building
☐ Energizer ☐ Review
☑ Communication ☐ Topical:

■ **Purpose:** To improve communication between trainees as well as their understanding of one another's roles back on the job.

■ **Time Required:** 90 minutes.

■ **Size of Group:** Unlimited.

■ **Materials Required:** Feedback sheets for each participant, prepared in advance by the trainer.

■ **The Exercise in Action:** Members of a work group who think they know each other well can improve their understanding of each others' roles with an exercise used by Mary Kate Pung, staff development specialist for Guilford County, NC. The exercise takes about 90 minutes and is especially effective for staff meetings or retreats.

A few days before the meeting, participants receive the following directions: Write a job description for yourself that includes the various roles you play on the job. Also write a success story that happened to you while on the job and a frustration you encountered. Don't spend more than 30 minutes on this project, and remember to bring enough copies for your coworkers to the meeting.

Pung prepares a large "feedback sheet" for each participant and divides it into thirds. Headings for the three sections are "Roles," "Successes," and "Frustrations."

During the session, participants sit in a circle or a U-shape configuration. Pung then passes out a feedback sheet to the person sitting to the right of the individual named on the sheet, so that each person in the group is holding someone else's feedback sheet.

Participants receive these instructions:

▼ Jot down one or two roles you believe the individual named on the sheet plays.

▼ Jot down one success story for the person named.

▼ Jot down one thing you think must be a frustration to them.

▼ Pass your paper to the right. Jot down some ideas for each person until you've done so for everyone in the group but yourself.

▼ Remember the Golden Rule: What kind of information would *you* like to receive?

When each person receives their own list, they have comments about perceptions of their roles, successes, and frustrations. After the feedback sheets are received, participants are given a chance to share with the group copies of their homework assignments (with descriptions of their roles, successes, and frustrations), reactions to the feedback they received, and any part of their roles they would like to change.

Pung says she's used the exercise with many work groups and it's always well-received. Sometimes, she says, participants are surprised at how well their roles are understood by coworkers.

**Game
Categories:**

☐ Opener
☐ Energizer
☐ Communication

☐ Team-building
☑ Review
☐ Topical:

■ **Purpose:** To review a lot of material, reward individual initiative, and at the same time allow each person to participate on a team.

■ **Time Required:** 15 minutes.

■ **Size of Group:** Unlimited.

■ **Materials Required:** Flip-chart paper and markers.

■ **The Exercise in Action:** Taking your class "to the races" is a fun and inexpensive way to review material. Here's how it works:

Tape two pieces of flip-chart paper end to end with the short ends touching. Then draw a racetrack and divide it into 10 sections, one for each review question. You can have as few as two teams, or as many as five, comfortably.

The action begins as you ask questions to advance the "horses." If the question is answered correctly by the individual whose turn it is to answer for the team, the team's horse moves forward one square. If the question is answered incorrectly the horse moves back one square. If the individual doesn't think he or she can answer correctly, that person has the option of making it a group question. If the group then answers correctly, the horse stays in its place. If the group answers incorrectly, the horse moves back two squares.

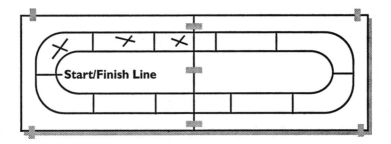

To create a "racetrack" review, tape two pieces of flip-chart paper end to end with the short ends touching. Then draw a racetrack and divide it into 10 sections, one for each review question.

TIP #93: Silent Brainstorming

Game   ☐ **Opener**   ☐ **Team-building**
Categories: ☐ **Energizer**   ☐ **Review**
                  ☑ **Communication**   ☐ **Topical:**

■ **Purpose:** To creatively encourage brainstorming among participants.

■ **Time Required:** 10-25 minutes.

■ **Size of Group:** Unlimited.

■ **Materials Required:** Post-it Notes.

■ **The Exercise in Action:** It's sometimes tough to get participants into the speak-without-filtering spirit of brainstorming, Julia Ballmer says, because they're accustomed to being careful about what they say in front of others. To encourage participation, she uses a "silent brainstorming" technique.

Ballmer, a sales representative with American Cyanamid, Madison, WI, gives each participant Post-it Notes, with instructions to address the problem as many ways as possible, and to record just one idea on each note. The method's anonymity lets people offer ideas they might not have offered orally, she says, and allows for the contribution of far more ideas in a smaller time frame.

Ballmer then asks them to post their ideas randomly on a classroom wall (or flip chart if the group is a small one). When all the ideas are posted, she asks participants to begin categorizing them by hand, without speaking. In this way, students are exposed to one another's ideas while developing a sense of structure for the conversation that follows.

TIP #94: Snowball Fight

Game Categories:	☐ Opener	☐ Team-building
	☐ Energizer	☐ Review
	☐ Communication	☑ Topical: Evaluation

■ **Purpose:** To garner anonymous course feedback.

■ **Time Required:** 10 minutes.

■ **Size of Group:** Unlimited.

■ **Materials Required:** Scrap paper for everyone.

■ **The Exercise in Action:** Getting honest feedback is an issue for every trainer, says William Weech, a foreign service office/course manager with the Foreign Service Institute, Arlington, VA. For that reason, he uses the "snowball" technique to gather what he hopes is better, more accurate input from attendees — on an anonymous basis.

Weech tells participants their input will be anonymous, and that he would like each person to neatly print three positive things about the course and three things needing improvement on a sheet of paper. After about three minutes, he asks participants to wad their papers into balls and have a "snowball fight." When the sheets are thoroughly randomized, he asks each student to pick up one sheet and read it to the class.

Says Weech: "The nice thing is that it allows everyone's voice to be heard without attribution. People can see what the general feeling of the group is without knowing specifically who thinks what." Often the exercise "snowballs" into a further discussion of what did and did not work during the session. And it ensures 100 percent participation in the evaluation process.

A final thought Weech keeps in mind during his presentations: Listen to trainees during a course and they'll evaluate you openly at the end. If they're convinced you don't listen, they won't bother to say much. In other words, don't wait until the end of a session to ask for (and respond to) feedback.

TIP #95: Up on Your Soapbox

Game Categories:
- ☐ Opener
- ☐ Energizer
- ☐ Communication
- ☑ Team-building
- ☐ Review
- ☐ Topical:

■ **Purpose:** To help attendees defuse difficult group conflicts and encourage team solutions.

■ **Time Required:** 15 minutes.

■ **Size of Group:** Unlimited, but trainees should work in small groups of four to eight.

■ **Materials Required:** A soft, indoor ball and a box of laundry detergent.

■ **The Exercise in Action:** To help training groups solve interpersonal conflicts, Bruce Lancia, a computer trainer with Wright-Patterson Air Force Base in Dayton, OH, uses a metaphorical "soap box" and a Nerf ball. It's essentially a "control measure to help groups meet project deadlines and to resolve gridlock," he says, and is also designed for use back on the job.

Each trainee group is given a soap box (such as a box Tide detergent) and a soft, indoor ball (such as a Nerf ball). When any conflict arises — usually over how to proceed in tasks — each participant is allotted a certain amount of time to be on the proverbial soapbox to state her perspective on the problem. "And if anyone feels that one opinion is being beaten to death, and it's a minority opinion, they have the right to grab the Nerf, and throw it at the individual on the soapbox," Lancia says. When a speaker is "Nerfed," says Lancia, they have the right to appeal to the group for more time. If a majority says, "No," they have to relinquish their post.

TIP #96: Teddy Bears and Computers?

Game Categories:	☐ Opener	☐ Team-building
	☐ Energizer	☐ Review
	☐ Communication	☑ Topical: Computer

■ **Purpose:** To enhance memory of technical information in computer classes.

■ **Time Required:** 10 minutes.

■ **Size of Group:** Unlimited.

■ **Materials Required:** 12 small teddy bears.

■ **The Exercise in Action:** To enhance memory of the functions of 12 computer keys specific to newly-implemented software, Janice Smith, a trainer with the Texas Rehabilitation Commission in Austin, TX, uses the venerable teddy bear — albeit in small version — as a retention tool and temporary reward for performance.

After initial instruction is completed, participants are asked to select the function key they feel will be most useful/important to their specific job tasks. As they answer, a miniature teddy bear with jointed arms and legs, purchased at a local discount store, is given to them by the trainer to sit near their monitors as a reminder of that key. The small bears have tiny cloth bibs made by Smith with the key and its particular function written on them.

At the end of class, Smith asks participants to return each "function key bear" for use in the next class.

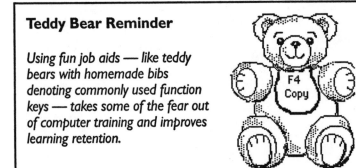

Teddy Bear Reminder

Using fun job aids — like teddy bears with homemade bibs denoting commonly used function keys — takes some of the fear out of computer training and improves learning retention.

F4
Copy

---

101 More Games for Trainers

Game Categories:	☐ Opener	☐ Team-building
	☐ Energizer	☐ Review
	☐ Communication	☑ Topical: Evaluation

■ **Purpose:** To take trainees' "temperature" and help the instructor deliver hot training.

■ **Time Required:** 10 minutes.

■ **Size of Group:** Unlimited.

■ **Materials Required:** Colored sticky dots. A thermometer drawn on flip-chart paper.

■ **The Exercise in Action:** End-of-session evaluation forms are nice for the instructor and for future students, but they don't do much to improve the session for the attendees who fill them out at the end of a course. Colleen McCarthy, an educator at Markham-Stoussville Hospital, Markham, Ontario, gets feedback throughout a session using sticky dots and a thermometer drawn on flip-chart paper.

Attendees are invited to use color-coded stickers during breaks to mark how "hot" or "cold" she is on various course components. For example, if McCarthy asks students to gauge the relevance of the course so far, students can place a blue sticker near the bottom of the thermometer if they feel the course is "cool" or a little off base so far; similarly, when asked to rate her delivery of material, a red sticker might be used to show she's "hot" and doing well.

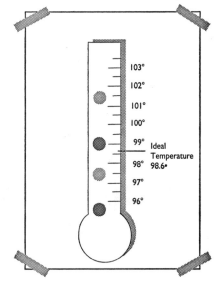

To make the thermometer even more telling, mark an "ideal temperature" near the midpoint. Then students can place dots denoting either too much or too little. For example, a student who believes the materials are being covered too rapidly might place a dot at the extreme top of the thermometer, not necessarily meaning that the delivery is hot and right on target, while a person who feels delivery is too slow may place a dot near the low end of the scale.

TIP #98: What's Wrong with this Picture?

Game Categories:

☐ Opener   ☐ Team-building
☐ Energizer   ☐ Review
☐ Communication   ☑ Topical: Problem-solving

■ **Purpose:** To provide a visual method for trainees to use to solve existing workplace problems.

■ **Time Required:** 15 to 20 minutes.

■ **Size of Group:** Unlimited.

■ **Materials Required:** Photos of existing conditions in a company.

■ **The Exercise in Action:** Cheryl Medlyn, with retailer Crabtree and Evelyn, says merchandising and display is crucial to her organization's success. In her training programs she uses photographs, and the approach of "What's wrong with this picture?"

The photographs allow trainee teams to analyze actual store arrangements and suggest changes or improvements without leaving the classroom. Medlyn says the exercise could be used in any problem-solving course where trainees are trying to solve existing workplace problems.

By blowing up and tracing the photos, teams can cut and paste new arrangements without having to redraw or cut the original photographs.

Game	☐ Opener	☐ Team-building
Categories:	☐ Energizer	☑ Review
	☐ Communication	☐ Topical:

■ **Purpose:** To creatively help participants remember technical information.

■ **Time Required:** 10 to 15 minutes.

■ **Size of Group:** Unlimited.

■ **Materials Required:** None.

■ **The Exercise in Action:** Using sound-alike terms and accompanying visual images can be one of the best ways to help participants remember difficult terminology, says Janice Bennett, a staff development instructor with Guthrie Healthcare System in Sayre, PA. She uses the technique to help her classes learn 350 medical terms in a basic medical terminology class.

For example, the term "emesis" sounds like "Hey, Mrs." and means "to vomit," so Bennett uses a two-part visual to help participants remember the chain reaction that causes emesis. Participants first see a woman and a bell hop in a hotel lobby, and in part two of the picture the woman is vomiting in the lobby and the bellhop is yelling, "Hey, Mrs.! You can't vomit in the lobby!"

As a review, she Bennett uses a takeoff on the game, "Win, Lose, or Draw." She first draws a picture of a particular medical element, and participants then have to identify the term, the sound-alike term, and the meaning after she completes the drawing.

Game Categories:	☑ **Opener**	☐ **Team-building**
	☑ **Energizer**	☐ **Review**
	☐ **Communication**	☐ **Topical:**

■ **Purpose:** To get people talking, and give students an unusual and interesting topic of conversation for their first course break.

■ **Time Required:** 15 minutes.

■ **Size of Group:** Unlimited.

■ **Materials Required:** Drawing utensils and paper for all participants.

■ **The Exercise in Action:** If the Myers-Briggs Personality Indicator leaves you cold, try a substitute: the Pig Personality Profile. It may not be sound science, he says, but it's good for a lot of laughs and effectively breaks the ice, says Gordon Cotton.

Cotton, a trainer at Marine Atlantic Inc., Monchton, New Brunswick, gives students the following instructions: "On a blank piece of paper, draw a pig. Don't look at your neighbors' pigs. Don't even glance." He provides no further guidance and does not explain the purpose of the exercise. (Note: You may find it interesting to follow the above instructions before reading the rest of this exercise.)

When participants are finished, he shares his tongue-in-cheek explanation that the pig serves as a useful test of the personality traits of the artist. He tells the class if the pig is drawn:

▼ Toward the top of the paper, you are a positive, optimistic person.

▼ Toward the middle of the page (top to bottom), you are a realist.

▼ Toward the bottom of the page, you are pessimistic and have a tendency to behave negatively.

▼ Facing left, you believe in tradition, are friendly, and remember dates, including birthdays.

▼ Facing forward (looking toward you) you are direct, enjoy playing devil's advocate, and neither fear nor avoid discussions.

▼ Facing right, you are innovative and active, but don't have a strong sense of family, nor do you remember dates.

▼ With many details, you are analytical, cautious, and distrustful.

▼ With few details, you are emotional and naive; you care little for details and are a risk-taker.

▼ With four legs showing, you are secure, stubborn, and stick to your ideals.

▼ With less than four legs showing, you are insecure, or are living through a period of major change.

▼ Further, the size of the pig's ears indicate how good a listener the artist is — large is good. And the length of the pig's tail — again, more is better — indicates the quality of the artist's sex life.

Says Cotton: "I won't attest to the accuracy of the results, other than to guarantee some laughter and amusement. I have delivered this test to about 400 participants and haven't offended anyone yet."

How and where training participants draw a pig on a blank piece of paper can provide humorous insights to their personalities. For example, because this pig was drawn near the top of the page, the artist is a positive, optimistic person. And because the pig is facing left, the artist believes in tradition, is friendly, and remembers dates.

TIP #101: Deadly Jelly Beans

Game Categories:	☐ Opener	☐ Team-building
	☐ Energizer	☐ Review
	☐ Communication	☑ Topical: Safety

■ **Purpose:** To give attendees of safety training classes a greater understanding of workplace accident statistics.

■ **Time Required:** 10 minutes.

■ **Size of Group:** Unlimited.

■ **Materials Required:** A large jar filled with several hundred jelly beans.

■ **The Exercise in Action:** It's not unusual for attendees in safety training classes to arrive with some "attitude," says Laurie Wainen, a safety process coordinator with Instrument Specialties, Delaware Water Gap, PA. "They believe they'll be the lucky ones who never have an accident at work," she says. "They've been doing something a certain way for years, and nothing's ever happened."

To open their often-jaded eyes to accident probabilities, she uses this exercise. First, she flashes statistics on an overhead about how many accidents happen each year on the job. Then she brings out a large jar filled with 300 jelly beans. She tells the class that she's injected 30 of the beans with a strong laxative, and to one bean she's added arsenic. Next, she asks trainees if they'd like to "reach in and grab one." Even the biggest thrill seekers beg off.

The apportionment of beans match the statistics: for every 300 possible hazard situations, there are 30 accidents (laxative) and one fatality (arsenic). Wainen's point? Trainees take the same chances every day by not wearing the right safety equipment or taking necessary safety precautions.

Robert Pike has been developing and imple-menting training programs for business, industry, government, and other professions since 1969. As president of Creative Training Techniques International Inc., Resources for Organizations Inc., and The Resources Group Inc., he leads more than 150 sessions each year on topics such as leadership, attitudes, motiva-tion, communication, decision-making, problem-solving, personal and organizational effective-ness, conflict management, team-building, and managerial productivity.

More than 50,000 trainers have attended Pike's Creative Training Techniques workshops. As a consult-ant, he has worked with such organizations as American Express, Upjohn, Hallmark Cards Inc., IBM, PSE&G, Bally's Casino Resort, and Shell Oil. A member of the American Society for Training and Develop-ment (ASTD) since 1972, he has served on three of the organization's national design groups, and held office as director of special interest groups and as a member of the national board.

An outstanding speaker, Pike has been a presenter at regional and national conferences for ASTD and other organizations. He currently serves as co-chairman of the Professional Emphasis Groups for the National Speakers' Association. He has been granted the professional designation of Certified Speaking Professional (CSP) by the NSA, an endorsement earned by only 170 of the organization's 3,800 members.

Pike is editor of Lakewood Publications' *Creative Training Techniques Newsletter*, author of *The Creative Training Techniques Handbook*, and has contributed articles to *TRAINING Magazine, The Personnel Administrator*, and *Self-Development Journal*. He has been listed, since 1980, in *Who's Who in the Midwest* and is listed in *Who's Who in Finance and Industry*.

WANT MORE COPIES?

This and most other Lakewood books are available at special quantity discounts when purchased in bulk. For details, write: Lakewood Books, 50 South Ninth St., Minneapolis, MN 55402. Call (800) 707-7769 or (612) 333-0471. Or fax your request to (612) 333-6526.

OTHER LAKEWOOD PUBLICATIONS

Creative Training Techniques Handbook, 2nd Edition..........$49.95

Powerful Audiovisual Techniques: 101 Ideas to Increase the Impact and Effectiveness of Your Training*......................$14.95

Motivating Your Trainees: 101 Proven Ways to Analyze Training Needs — And Get Results!*................................$14.95

Dynamic Openers & Energizers: 101 Tips and Tactics for Enlivening Your Training Classroom* $14.95

Optimizing Training Transfer: 101 Techniques for Improving Training Retention and Application*.............$14.95

Creative Training Tools: 101 Easy-to-Use Ideas for Increasing Trainee Participation*.......................................$14.95

Creative Training Techniques Newsletter (12 issues per year) $99.00

*Package price for all six "101" books listed above $69.95

TO ORDER, CONTACT: Lakewood Books, 50 South Ninth St., Minneapolis, MN 55402. Call (800) 707-7769 or (612) 333-0471. Fax (612) 333-6526.

UNCONDITIONAL GUARANTEE

Examine and use any of the resources on this page for a full 30 days. If you are not completely satisfied, for any reason whatsoever, simply return them and receive a full refund of the purchase price.